Our Best Knit Collection

Leisure Arts Inc. • Maumelle, Arkansas

Table of Contents

7
6

8

11

1. WOMEN'S PULLOVER

Size:	32	34	36	38	40
Chest Measurement:	32"	34"	36"	38"	40"
Finished Chest Measurement:	36"	38"	40"	42"	44"

Size Note: Instructions are written with sizes 32 and 34 in the first set of braces { } and with sizes 36, 38, and 40 in the second set of braces. Instructions will be easier to read if you circle all the numbers pertaining to your size. If only one number in given,
it applies to all sizes.

MATERIALS

Worsted Weight Yarn: MEDIUM 4
{17-18}{19-21-22} ounces,
[{480-510}{540-600-620} grams,
{985-1,045}{1,100-1,220-1,275} yards**]**
Straight knitting needles, sizes 5 (3. 75 mm) **and** 7 (4.50 mm) **or** sizes needed for gauge
16" Circular needle, size 5 (3. 75 mm)
Stitch holders - 2
Markers
Yarn needle

GAUGE: With large size needles,
in Stockinette Stitch, 20 sts and 26 rows = 4"

BACK
RIBBING

With small size needles,
cast on {92-98}{102-108-112} sts **loosely**.

Work in K1, P1 ribbing for 2".

BODY

Change to large size needles.

Work in Stockinette Stitch until Back measures approximately {19-19}{20-21-21}" from cast on edge, ending by working a **knit** row.

SHOULDER SHAPING

Rows 1 and 2: Bind off {10-11}{11-12-13} sts at the beginning of the next 2 rows, work across: {72-76}{80-84-86} sts.

Rows 3 and 4: Bind off {10-11}{12-12-13} sts at the beginning of the next 2 rows, work across: {52-54}{56-60-60} sts.

Rows 5 and 6: Bind off {11-12}{12-13-13} sts at the beginning of the next 2 rows, work across: {30-30}{32-34-34} sts.

Slip remaining sts onto st holder; cut yarn.

FRONT

Work same as Back until Front measures approximately {16½-16½{17-18-18}" from cast on edge, ending by working a **knit** row.

NECK SHAPING

Note: Both sides of Neck are worked at the same time, using separate yarn for **each** side.

Row 1: Purl {37-40}{41-43-45} sts, slip next {18-18}{20-22-22} sts onto st holder; with second yarn, purl across: {37-40}{41-43-45} sts **each** side.

Row 2 (Decrease row)**:** Knit across to within 2 sts of Neck edge, K2 tog ***(Fig. 6, page 44)***; with second yarn, slip 1 as if to **knit**, K1, PSSO ***(Figs. 8a & b, page 44)***, knit across: {36-39}{40-42-44} sts **each** side.

Row 3 (Decrease row)**:** Purl across to within 2 sts of Neck edge, P2 tog ***(Fig. 11, page 45)***; with second yarn P2 tog, purl across: {35-38}{39-41-43} sts **each** side.

Row 4 (Decrease row)**:** Knit across to within 2 sts of Neck edge, K2 tog; with second yarn, slip 1 as if to **knit**, K1, PSSO, knit across: {34-37}{38-40-42} sts **each** side.

Row 5: Purl across; with second yarn, purl across.

Rows 6-11: Repeat Rows 4 and 5, 3 times: {31-34}{35-37-39} sts **each** side.

Work even until Front measures same as Back to Shoulder Shaping, ending by working a **purl** row.

SHOULDER SHAPING

Rows 1 and 2: Bind off {10-11}{11-12-13} sts at Armhole edge, work across; with second yarn, work across: {21-23}{24-25-26} sts **each** side.

Rows 3 and 4: Bind off {10-11}{12-12-13} sts at Armhole edge, work across; with second yarn, work across: {11-12}{12-13-13} sts **each** side.

Row 5: Bind off {11-12}{12-13-13} sts; with second yarn, knit across.

Bind off remaining sts.

SLEEVE (Make 2)
RIBBING

With small size needles, cast on {46-50}{52-52-52} sts **loosely**.

Work in K1, P1 ribbing for 2½".

BODY

Change to large size needles.

Row 1 (Right side)**:** Knit across.

Row 2: Purl across.

Row 3 (Increase row)**:** K1, increase ***(Figs. 3a & b,page 43)***, knit across to last 2 sts, increase, K1: {48-52}{54-54-54} sts.

Working in Stockinette Stitch, continue to increase one stitch at **each** edge in same manner, every {4-4}{4-2-2} rows, {13-15}{17-2-5} times **more**; then increase every {6-6}{6-4-4} rows, {4-3}{2-20-19} times: {82-88}{92-98-102} sts.

Work even until Sleeve measures approximately {16¼-17}{17¼ -17½-17¼}" from cast on edge or desired length to underarm, ending by working a **purl** row.

SLEEVE CAP

Bind off 5 sts at the beginning of the next {14-16}{16-18-18} rows, work across: {12-8}{12-8-12} sts.

Bind off remaining sts.

FINISHING

Sew shoulder seams.

NECK RIBBING

With **right** side facing and using circular needles, knit {30-30}{32-34-34} sts from Back st holder, pick up {21-22}{24-24-24} sts along left Front Neck edge ***(Fig. 14a, page 46)***, knit {18-18}{20-22-22} sts from Front st holder, pick up {21-22}{24-24-24} sts along right Front Neck edge, place marker for beginning of rnd ***(see Markers, page 43)***: {90-92}{100-104-104} sts.

Work in K1, P1 ribbing around for 1".

Bind off all sts **loosely** in ribbing.

Sew Sleeves to sweater, matching center of last row on Sleeve to shoulder seam and beginning {8½-9}{9½-10-10½}" down from seam.

Weave underarm and side in one continuous seam ***(Fig. 15, page 46)***.

---

2. SCARF

Finished Size: 7"w x 60"l

MATERIALS

Bulky Weight Yarn:
- Red - 5 ounces, (140 grams, 225 yards)
- Blue - 3 ounces, (90 grams, 135 yards)

Straight knitting needles, size 9 (5.5 mm) **or** size needed for gauge
Cable needle
Bobbin

GAUGE: In Stockinette Stitch, 16 sts and 21 rows= 4"

STITCH GUIDE

FRONT CABLE (uses next 3 sts)
Slip next st onto cable needle and hold in **front** of work, K2 from left needle, K1 from cable needle.

BACK CABLE (uses next 3 sts)
Slip next 2 sts onto cable needle and hold in **back** of work, K1 from left needle, K2 from cable needle.

Note: Wind bobbin with Red. Always keep the bobbin on the wrong side of the Scarf. When changing colors, always pick up the new color from beneath the dropped yarn and keep the color which has just been worked to the left ***(Fig. C, page 12)***.

With Red, cast on 33 sts **loosely**.

Row 1: K1, (P1, K1) across.

Row 2: P1, (K1, P1) across.

Rows 3-6: Repeat Rows 1 and 2, twice.

Row 7 (Right side): (K1, P1) twice, with Blue K 25, with Red bobbin (P1, K1) twice.

Row 8: (P1, K1) twice, with Blue P 25, with Red (K1, P1) twice.

Row 9: (K1, P1) twice, K5, (slip 1 as if to **knit**, K3) 5 times, (P1, K1) twice.

Row 10: (P1, K1) twice, (P3, slip 1 as if to **knit)** 5 times, P5, (K1, P1) twice.

Row 11: (K1, P1) twice, with Blue K3, work Back Cable, (K1, work Back Cable) 4 times, K3, with Red (P1, K1) twice.

Row 12: (P1, K1) twice, with Blue P 25, with Red (K1, P1) twice.

Row 13: (K1, P1) twice, K1, (slip 1 as if to **purl**, K3) 6 times, (P1, K1) twice.

Row 14: (P1, K1) twice, (P3, slip 1 as if to **purl**) 6 times, P1, (K1, P1) twice.

Row 15: (K1, P1) twice, with Blue K1, (work Front Cable, K1) 6 times, with Red (P1, K1) twice.

Repeat Rows 8-15 until Scarf measures approximately 59" from cast on edge, ending by working Row 12.

Last 6 Rows: Repeat Rows 1-6.

Bind off all sts **loosely** in ribbing.

3. GOLF CLUB COVERS

MATERIALS
Worsted Weight Yarn: MEDIUM 4
Grey - 5 ounces, (140 grams, 315 yards)
Red - 2 ounces, (60 grams, 125 yards)
Straight knitting needles, sizes 6 (4 mm) **and** 7 (4.5 mm) **or** sizes needed for gauge
Yarn needle

GAUGE: With large size needles, in Stockinette Stitch, 10 sts and 13 rows = 2"

COVER (Make 4)
RIBBING
With small size needles and Grey, cast on 36 sts **loosely**.

Work in K2, P2 ribbing for 5" increasing 5 sts evenly spaced across last row ***(see Increases, page 43)***: 41 sts.

BODY
Change to large size needles.

Beginning with a **knit** row, work in Stockinette Stitch until Cover measures approximately 10¾" from cast on edge.

Cut yarn leaving an 18" end for sewing. Thread yarn needle with yarn end and separately slip each stitch from the knitting needle onto the yarn; gather the stitches **tightly** and secure end.

FINISHING
Each Grey square on the charts represents one Duplicate Stitch. Using Red and following Charts, Duplicate Stitch a number to center of each Cover, beginning at bottom of number and 1" above Ribbing as follows:

Each knit stitch forms a "V" and you want to completely cover that "V" Bring your needle up from the **wrong** side at the base of the "V", leaving a 6" end to be woven in later. Follow the right side of the "V" up and insert the needle under the legs of the "V" immediately above it ***(Fig. A)***. Follow the left side of the "V" back down to the base, amd insert the needle where you started this stitch ***(Fig. B)***.

Repeat for all Duplicate stitches, keeping tension even with tension of knitted fabric to avoid puckering. Duplicate Stitch will cover best if you change direction (right to left and left to right) on alternate rows.

Fig. A

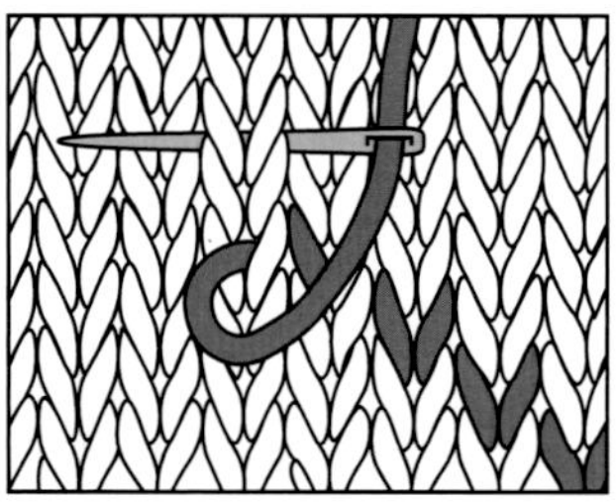

Fig. B

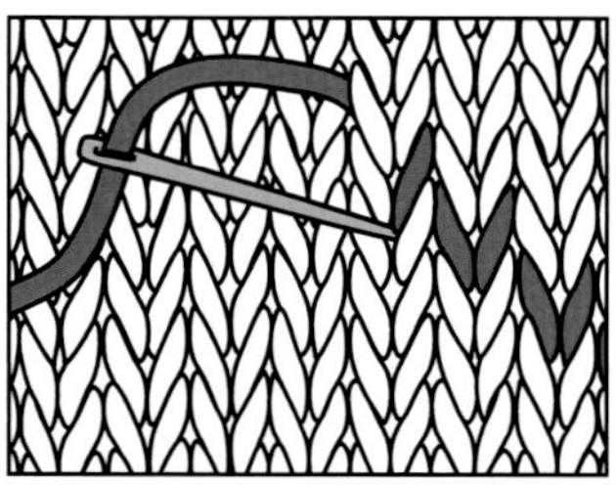

CHARTS

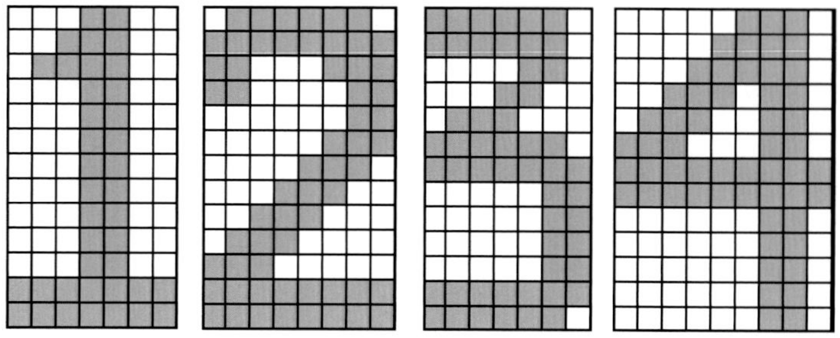

Weave seam ***(Fig 15, page 46)***.

Using Grey and Red, make Pom-Pom ***(Figs. 16a-c, page 46)***.

Sew Pom-Pom to top of Cover.

4. DICKEYS

Finished Size: 10½" wide

MATERIALS
Sport Weight Yarn: LIGHT 3
2¾ ounces, (80 grams, 275 yards) **each**
Straight knitting needles, size 6 (4 mm) **or** size needed for gauge
16" Circular needle, size 5 (3.75 mm)
Stitch holder
Marker

MOSS STRIPES
Shown at the top of photo, page 25.

GAUGE: With large size needles, in Stockinette Stitch, 22 sts = 4"

FRONT
With large size needles, cast on 60 sts **loosely**.

Row 1 (Right side)**:** Knit across.

Row 2: (K1, P1) across.

Row 3: Knit across.

Row 4: (P1, K1) across.

Rows 5-20: Repeat Rows 1-4, 4 times.

Rows 21-30: Work in Stockinette Stitch for 10 rows.

Rows 31-40: Repeat Rows 1-4 twice, then repeat Rows 1 and 2 once **more**.

Rows 41-80: Repeat Rows 21-40 twice.

NECK SHAPING

Row 1: K 45, slip last 30 sts worked onto st holder, knit across: 15 sts **each** side.

Note: Both sides of Neck are worked at the same time, using separate yarn for **each** side.

Row 2: Purl across; with second yarn, purl across.

Row 3 (Decrease row)**:** Knit across to within 2 sts of Neck edge, K2 tog ***(Fig. 6, page 44)***; with second yarn, slip 1 as if to **knit**, K1, PSSO ***(Figs. 8a & b, page 44)***, knit across: 14 sts **each** side.

Rows 4-7: Repeat Rows 2 and 3 twice: 12 sts **each** side.

Work even in Stockinette Stitch until Neck measures approximately 3", ending by working a **knit** row.

Next Row: Purl across, add on 36 sts **loosely *(Figs. 5a & b, page 43)***, **turn**; with same yarn, purl across; cut unused yarn: 60 sts.

BACK

Row 1: Knit across.

Row 2: (K1, P1) across.

Row 3: Knit across.

Row 4: (P1, K1) across.

Rows 5-10: Repeat Rows 1-4 once, then repeat Rows 1 and 2 once **more**.

Rows 11-20: Work in Stockinette Stitch for 10 rows.

Rows 21-80: Repeat Rows 1-20 twice; then repeat Rows 1-4, 5 times.

Bind off all sts **loosely**.

NECK RIBBING

With **right** side facing, using circular needle and starting at center Back, pick up 18 sts across left Back Neck edge ***(Figs. 14a & b, page 46)***, pick up 17 sts along left Neck edge, knit 30 sts from st holder, pick up 17 sts along right Neck edge, pick up 18 sts across right Back Neck edge, place marker to indicate the beginning of the rnd ***(see Markers, page 43)***: 100 sts.

Work in K1, P1 ribbing for 12 rounds.

Bind off all sts **loosely** in ribbing.

HERRINGBONE

Shown at the bottom of photo, page 25.

GAUGE: With large size needles, in pattern, 21 sts = 3½"

STITCH GUIDE

INCREASE

Insert the right needle from the **front** into the side of the stitch **below** the next stitch on the left needle ***(Fig. A)*** and knit it.

Fig. A

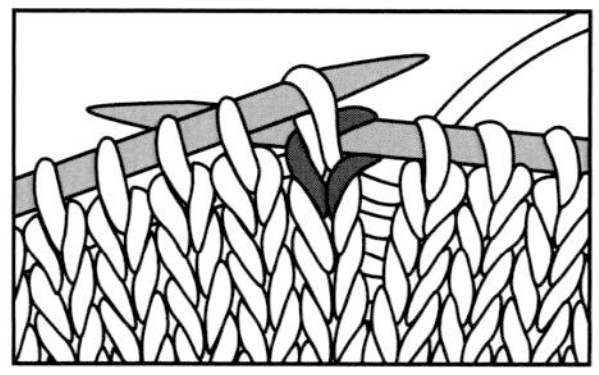

FRONT

With large size needles, cast on 64 sts **loosely**.

Row 1: Purl across.

Row 2 (Right side)**:** K2 tog ***(Fig. 6, page 44)***, K2, increase ***(Fig. A)***, ★ K3, K2 tog, K2, increase; repeat from ★ across to last 4 sts, K4.

Row 3: Purl across.

Row 4: K3, increase, K3, K2 tog, ★ K2, increase, K3, K2 tog; repeat from ★ across.

Rows 5-80: Repeat Rows 1-4, 19 times.

NECK SHAPING

Note: Both sides of Neck are worked at the same time, using separate yarn for **each** side.

Row 1: P 15, slip next 34 sts onto st holder; with second yarn, purl across: 15 sts **each** side.

Work even until Neck measures approximately 3", ending by working a **purl** row.

Next Row: Work across, add on 34 sts **loosely *(Figs. 5a & b, page 43)***, **turn**; with same yarn, work across; cut unused yarn: 64 sts.

BACK

Rows 1-80: Work across in pattern.

Bind off all sts **loosely**.

NECK RIBBING

With **right** side facing, using circular needle and starting at center Back, pick up 17 sts across left Back Neck edge ***(Figs. 14a & b, page 46)***, pick up 16 sts along left Neck edge, knit 34 sts from st holder, pick up 16 sts along right Neck edge, pick up 17 sts across right Back Neck edge, place marker to indicate the beginning of the rnd ***(see Markers, page 43)***: 100 sts.

Work in K1, P1 ribbing for 12 rounds.

Bind off all sts **loosely** in ribbing.

Designs by Carolyn Pfeifer.

5. ROMPER

Months (size):	6	12	18
Finished Chest Measurement:	24"	25½"	27"

Size Note: Instructions are written for size 6 months, with sizes 12 and 18 months in braces { }. Instuctions will be easier to read if you circle all the numbers pertaining to your size. If only one number is given, it applies to all sizes.

MATERIALS

100% Cotton Double Knitting Yarn: (LIGHT 3)
- Pink - 8{9-10} ounces, **[**230{260-280} grams, 525{590-660} yards**]**
- White - 1¾ ounces, (50 grams, 115 yards)
- Blue - 1¾ ounces, (50 grams, 115 yards)
- Yellow - 1¾ ounces, (50 grams, 115 yards)
- Green - 1¾ ounces, (50 grams, 115 yards)

Straight knitting needles, sizes 4 (3.5 mm), 5 (3.75 mm), **and** 6 (4 mm) **or** sizes needed for gauge
Stitch holders - 3
Yarn needle
½" Buttons - 5{5-6}

GAUGE: With large size needles, in Stockinette Stitch, 22 sts and 28 rows = 4"

LEFT FRONT
RIBBING

With medium size needles and White, cast on 22{24-26} sts **loosely**.

Work in K1, P1 ribbing for 7 rows.

BODY

Knit across increasing 12 sts evenly spaced ***(see Increases, page 43)***: 34{36-38} sts.

Change to large size needles.

Beginning with a **purl** row, work in Stockinette Stitch in the following Stripe Sequence: 6 Rows **each** of Pink, Blue, Yellow, and Green.

Change to Pink and work even until piece measures approximately 7½{8½-9½}" from cast on edge, ending by working a **knit** row.

PLACKET SHAPING

Row 1: Bind off 3 sts, purl across: 31{33-35} sts.

Work even until piece measures approximately 22{24-26}" from cast on edge, ending by working a **purl** row.

NECK SHAPING

Row 1: Knit across to last 6 sts, slip last 6 sts onto st holder: 25{27-29} sts.

Row 2: Purl across.

Row 3 (Decrease row)**:** Knit across to last 2 sts, K2 tog ***(Fig. 6, page 44)***: 24{26-28} sts.

Row 4: Purl across.

Rows 5-8: Repeat Rows 3 and 4 twice: 22{24-26} sts.

Bind off remaining sts.

RIGHT FRONT

Work same as Left Front to Placket Shaping, ending working a **purl** row: 34{36-38} sts.

PLACKET SHAPING

Row 1: Bind off 3 sts, knit across: 31{33-35} sts.

Work even until piece measures same as Left Front, ending by working a **knit** row.

NECK SHAPING

Row 1: Purl across to last 6 sts, slip last 6 sts onto second st holder: 25{27-29} sts.

Row 2 (Decrease row)**:** Slip 1 as if to **knit**, K1, PSSO ***(Figs. 8a & b, page 44)***, knit across: 24{26-28} sts.

Row 3: Purl across.

Rows 4-7: Repeat Rows 2 and 3 twice: 22{24-26} sts.

Bind off remaining sts.

BACK
LEFT LEG

Work same as Left Front until piece measures approximately 6{7-8}" from cast on edge, ending by working a **purl** row: 34{36-38} sts.

Slip all sts onto remaining st holder.

RIGHT LEG

Work same as Left Front until piece measures same as Left Leg, ending by working a **knit** row: 34{36-38} sts.

BODY

Joining Row: Slip sts from Left Leg st holder onto empty needle and knit across: 68{72-76} sts.

Work even until piece measures approximately 22½{24½-26½}" from cast on edge, ending by working a **knit** row.

NECK SHAPING

Note: Both sides of Neck are worked at the same time using separate yarn for **each** side.

Row 1: P 23{25-27}, slip next 22 sts onto remaining st holder; with second yarn, purl across: 23{25-27} sts **each** side.

Row 2: Knit across to within 2 sts of Neck edge, K2 tog; with second yarn, slip 1 as if to **knit**, K1, PSSO, knit across: 22{24-26} sts **each** side.

Row 3: Purl across; with second yarn, purl across.

Bind off remaining sts.

Sew shoulder seams.

SLEEVE
BODY
Place a marker on each side of Front and Back, 4½{5-5½}" down from shoulder seam.

With **right** side facing, using large size needles and Pink, pick up 50{56-60} sts evenly spaced between markers ***(Fig. 14a, page 46)***.

> ***Note:*** Work in the following Stripe Sequence: 3{7-11} Rows of Pink, 6 rows **each** of Green, Yellow, Blue, and Pink.

Row 1: Purl across.

Row 2: Knit across.

Row 3: Purl across.

Row 4 (Decrease row)**:** Slip 1 as if to **knit**, K1, PSSO, knit across to last 2 sts, K2 tog: 48{54-58} sts.

Continue to decrease one stitch at **each** edge, every fourth row, 5{5-7} times **more**; then decrease every other row, 1{3-1} time(s), ending by working a **purl** row: 36{38-42} sts.

RIBBING
Change to medium size needles and White.

Row 1: Knit across.

Work in K1, P1 ribbing for 7 rows.

Bind off all sts **loosely** in ribbing.

FINISHING
Weave underarm and side in one continuous seam ***(Fig. 15, page 46)***.
Sew inner leg seams to joining row of Back.
Sew Right Front to Left Front from joining row to Placket Shaping.

LEFT FRONT BAND
With right side facing, using small size needles and White, pick up 68{72-78} sts evenly spaced across Left Front.

Work in K1, P1 ribbing for 7 rows.

Bind off all sts loosely in ribbing.

RIGHT FRONT BAND
With **right** side facing, using small size needles and White, pick up 68{72-78} sts evenly spaced across Right Front.

Rows 1-3: (K1, P1) across.

Row 4 (Buttonhole row): K1, (P1, K1) 5{3-3} times, ★ YO ***(Fig. 13a, page 45)***, K2 tog, (P1, K1) 6{7-6} times; repeat from ★ across to last st, P1.

Rows 5-7: (K1, P1) across.

Bind off all sts loosely in ribbing.

Lapping Right Band over Left, sew bottom edges to bound off sts at Placket Shaping.

NECKBAND
With **right** side facing, using small size needles and White, pick up 7 sts along end of Right Front Band, knit 6 sts from Right Front st holder, pick up 8 sts along Right Front Neck edge, pick up 4 sts along Right Back Neck edge, knit 22 sts from Back st holder, pick up 4 sts along Left Back Neck edge, pick up 8 sts along Left Front Neck edge, slip 6 sts from Left Front st holder onto empty needle and knit across, pick up 7 sts along end of Left Front Band: 72 sts.

Rows 1 and 2: (K1, P1) across.

Row 3 (Buttonhole row)**:** (K1, P1) across to last 4 sts, K2 tog, YO, K1, P1.

Rows 4-6: (K1, P1) across.

Bind off all sts **loosely** in ribbing.

Sew buttons to Left Front Band.

Design by Carole Prior.

---

6. DISHCLOTH

Finished Size: 11" square

MATERIALS
100% Cotton Worsted Weight Yarn: MEDIUM 4
- Blue - 2 ounces, (60 grams, 90 yards)
- Ecru - ½ ounce, (20 grams, 25 yards)

Straight knitting needles, size 7 (4.5 mm) **or** size needed for gauge
Crochet hook, size E (3.5 mm)

GAUGE: In pattern, 4 sts = 1"

BODY
With Blue, cast on 44 sts.

Rows 1-4: Knit across.

Row 5 (Right side)**:** Drop Blue, with Ecru, K1,★ YO ***(Fig. 13a, page 45)***, K2 tog ***(Fig. 6, page 44)***; repeat from ★ across to last st, K1.

Row 6: Knit across; drop Ecru.

Rows 7-10: With Blue, knit across.

Rows 11-76: Repeat Rows 5-10, 11 times.

Cut Ecru; bind off all sts leaving remaining loop on needle; do **not** cut yarn.

EDGING
With right side facing, slip loop onto crochet hook, ch 1 ***(see Crochet Stitches, page 47)***, 3 sc in same st, sc evenly around working 3 sc in each corner; join with slip st to first sc, finish off.

Design by Eunice Svinicki.

7. POT HOLDER

Finished Size: 8"w x 7"h

MATERIALS

100% Cotton Worsted Weight Yarn: (MEDIUM 4)
Blue - 1¼ ounces, (35 grams, 60 yards)
Ecru - ½ ounce, (20 grams, 25 yards)
Straight knitting needles, size 7 (4.5 mm)
or size needed for gauge
Crochet hook, size E (3.50 mm)

GAUGE: In pattern, 4 sts = 1"

BODY (Make 2)

With Blue, cast on 32 sts.

Row 1 (Right side)**:** Knit across.

Row 2: Purl across.

Rows 3 and 4: Repeat Rows 1 and 2; at end of Row 4, drop Blue.

Rows 5 and 6: With Ecru, knit across.

Row 7: Drop Ecru, with Blue, K2, ★ with yarn in **back**, slip 1 as if to **purl**, K2: repeat from ★ across.

Row 8: K2, ★ with yarn in **front**, slip 1 as if to **purl**, K2; repeat from ★ across; drop Blue.

Rows 9 and 10: With Ecru, knit across.

Row 11: Drop Ecru, with Blue, knit across.

Rows 12-44: Repeat Rows 2-11, 3 times; then repeat Rows 2-4 once **more**.

Bind off all sts **loosely**.

JOINING

With **wrong** sides together, working through **both** pieces, and using crochet hook, join Blue with slip st in any corner ***(see Crochet Stitches, page 47)***; ch 1, 3 sc in same st, sc evenly around working 3 sc in each corner; join with slip st to first sc; ch 15, join with slip st to form a ring, turn; slip st in each ch around; finish off.

Design by Eunice Svinicki.

8. PILLOW

Finished Size: 14" square

MATERIALS

Worsted Weight Yarn: (MEDIUM 4)
Brown - 5 ounces, (140 grams, 305 yards)
Ecru - 2 ounces, (60 grams, 120 yards)
Straight knitting needles, size 7 (4.5 mm}
or size needed for gauge
14" Pillow form
Yarn needle

GAUGE: In pattern, 22 sts = 4";
in Stockinette Stitch, 20 sts and 26 rows =4"

FRONT

With Brown, cast on 81 sts **loosely**.

Row 1: Purl across.

Note: When instructed to slip a stitch, with yarn at **wrong** side, always slip as if to **purl**.

Row 2 (Right side)**:** Drop Brown, with Ecru, K1, slip 1, K1, (slip 3, K1) across to last 2 sts, slip 1, K1.

Row 3: P4, slip 1, (P3, slip 1) across to last 4 sts, P4.

Row 4: Drop Ecru, with Brown, K2, slip 1, (K3, slip 1) across to last 2 sts, K2.

Row 5: Purl across.

Row 6: Drop Brown, with Ecru, K1, (slip 3, K1) across.

Row 7: P2, slip 1, (P3, slip 1) across to last 2 sts, P2.

Row 8: Drop Ecru, with Brown, K4, slip 1, (K3, slip across to last 4 sts, K4.

Row 9: Purl across.

Row 10: Drop Brown, with Ecru, K1, slip 1, K1, (slip 3, K1) across to last 2 sts, slip 1, K1.

Repeat Rows 3-10 for pattern until Front measures approximately 14½" from cast on edge, ending by working a **purl** row.

Bind off all sts **loosely** in **knit**.

BACK

With Brown, cast on 73 sts **loosely**.

Beginning with a **purl** row, work in Stockinette Stitch until Back measures approximately 14½" from cast on edge, ending by working a **purl** row.

Bind off all sts **loosely** in **knit**.

FINISHING

With **wrong** sides of Front and Back together and using Brown, sew seam inserting pillow form before closing.

Design by Joyce Winfield Vanderslice.

9. SCARF CAP

Hat intended to fit head measurement, from shoulder to shoulder across top of head, of approximately 14" to 16".

MATERIALS

Worsted Weight Yarn: MEDIUM 4
- White - 5½ ounces, (160 grams, 365 yards)
- Green - 15 yards
- Yellow - 15 yards

Straight knitting needles, size 8 (5 mm) **or** size needed for gauge

Yarn needle

GAUGE: In Seed Stitch, 18 sts and 30 rows= 4"

Note: When instructed to slip a stitch, with yarn in **back**, always slip as if to **purl**.

RIGHT SCARF

With White, cast on 34 sts **loosely**.

Row 1: (K1, P1) across.

Rows 2-19: Slip 1, P1, (K1, P1) across.

Row 20 (Right side)**:** Cut White, with Green, knit across.

Rows 21-25: Slip 1, P1, (K1, P1) across.

Row 26: Cut Green, with White, knit across.

Rows 27-31: Slip 1, P1, (K1, P1) across.

Row 32: Cut White, with Yellow, knit across.

Rows 33-37: Slip 1, P1, (K1, P1) across.

Row 38: Cut Yellow, with White, knit across.

Repeat Row 2 until Scarf measures approximately 16" from last color change, ending by working a **wrong** side row.

CAP

Row 1: Bind off 7 sts **loosely** in ribbing, loop a short piece of yarn around last bound off st to mark Front Band placement, work across increasing 7 sts evenly spaced ***(see Increases, page 43)***: 34 sts.

Row 2: (K1, P1) across.

Row 3: (P1, K1) across.

Repeat Rows 2 and 3 for Seed St until Cap measures approximately 16", ending by working a **wrong** side row.

LEFT SCARF

Row 1: Add on 7 sts **loosely** ***(Figs. 5a & b, page 43)***, K1, (P1, K1) 3 times, loop a short piece of yarn around last st worked to mark Front Band placement, work across decreasing 7 sts evenly spaced ***(see Decreases, pages 44 & 45)***: 34 sts.

Row 2: Slip 1, P1, (K1, P1) across.

Repeat Row 2 until Scarf measures approximately 16" from Hood, ending by working a **wrong** side row.

STRIPES

Row 1: Cut White, with Yellow, knit across.

Rows 2-6: Slip 1, P1, (K1, P1) across.

Row 7: Cut Yellow, with White, knit across.

Rows 8-12: Slip 1, P1, (K1, P1) across.

Row 13: Cut White, with Green, knit across.

Rows 14-18: Slip 1, P1, (K1, P1) across.

Row 19: Cut Green, with White, knit across.

Rows 20-38: Slip 1, P1, (K1, P1) across.

Bind off all sts **loosely** in ribbing.

FINISHING

FRONT BAND

With **right** side facing and using White, pick up 78 sts evenly spaced between markers ***(Fig. 14a, page 46)***.

Work in K1, P1 ribbing for 1½".

Bind off all sts **loosely** in ribbing.

Sew edges of Front Band to Scarf.
Weave back seam of Cap from center to beginning of Scarf ***(Fig. 15, page 46)***.
Add Pom-Pom ***(Figs. 16a-c, page 46)***.

Design by Jocelyn Stricker.

10. STARS & STRIPES CAP

Hat intended to fit head measurement of approximately 18½" to 20" for size Small and 20" to 21½" for size Medium.

Size Note: Instructions are written for size Small with size Medium in braces { }. Instructions will be easier to read if you circle all the numbers pertaining to your size. If only one number is given, it applies to both sizes.

MATERIALS

Worsted Weight Yarn:
- White - 1{1½} ounce(s), [30{40} grams, 70{100) yards]
- Red - 1{1½} ounce(s), [30{40} grams, 70{100} yards]
- Blue - ½{1} ounce, [20{30} grams, 35{70} yards]

Straight knitting needles, sizes 5 (3. 75 mm) **and** 7 (4.5 mm) **or** sizes needed for gauge
Purchased Star Appliqués
Yarn needle

GAUGE: With large size needles, in Stockinette Stitch, 20 sts and 26 rows = 4"

STITCH GUIDE

THROUGH BACK LOOP

When instructed to knit into the back loop of stitch ***(Fig. A)***, the result will be twisted stitches ***(Fig. B)***.

Fig. A

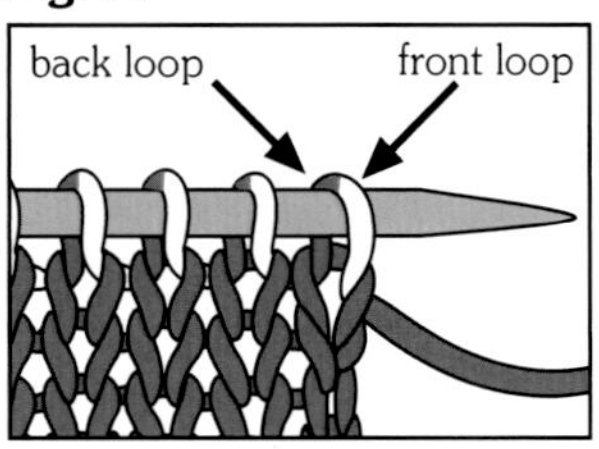

Fig B

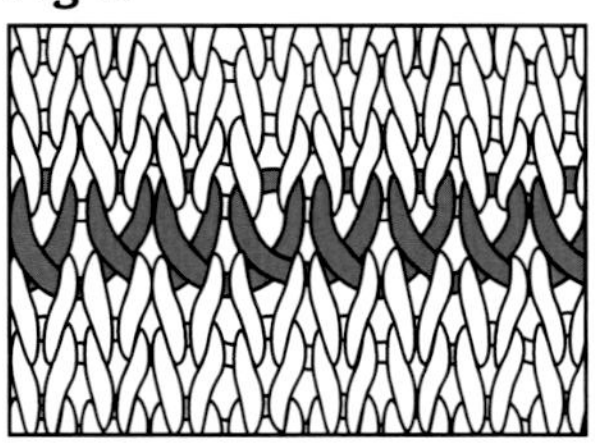

CHANGING COLORS

When changing colors, always pick up the new color yarn from **beneath** the dropped yarn and keep the color which has just been worked to the left of the new yarn ***(Fig. C)*** this will prevent holes in the finish piece. Take extra care to keep your tension even. Carry unused yarn **loosely** across back of work ***(Fig. D)***.

Fig C

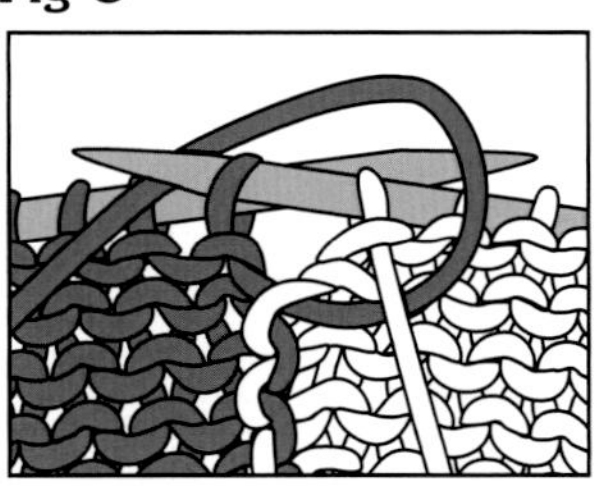

Fig. D

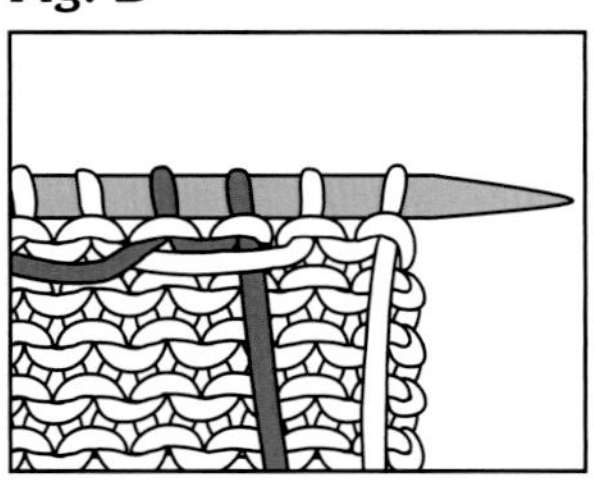

TWISTED RIBBING

With small size needles and Blue, cast on 92{98} sts **loosely**.

Rows 1-11: ★ K1 through back loop ***(Figs. A & B)***, P1; repeat from ★ across.

CROWN

Change to large size needles.

Row 1 (Right side)**:** With Red K1,★ with White K3 ***(Figs. C & D)***, with Red K3; repeat from ★ across to last st, with White K1.

Row 2: P2, (with Red P3, with White P3) across.

Row 3: K2, (with Red K3, with White K3) across.

Row 4: With Red P1, (with White P3, with Red P3) across to last st, with White P1.

Row 5: (With Red K3, with White K3) across to last 2 sts, with Red K2.

Row 6: (With Red P3, with White P3) across to last 2 sts, with Red P2.

Rows 7-25{31}: Repeat Rows 1-6, 3{4} times; then repeat Row 1 once **more**; cut Red.

SHAPING

Row 1: Purl across.

Row 2: K2{1}, K2 tog across to last 2{1} st(s) ***(Fig. 6, page 44)***, K2{1}: 48{50} sts.

Row 3: Purl across.

Row 4: K2{1}, K2 tog across to last 2{1} st(s), K2{1}: 26 sts.

Row 5: Purl across.

Row 6: K1, K2 tog across to last st, K1: 14 sts.

Rows 7-10: Repeat Rows 5 and 6 twice: 5 sts.

Cut White leaving an 18" end for sewing.

FINISHING

Thread yarn needle with yarn end and separately slip each stitch from the knitting needle onto the yarn; gather the stitches **tightly** and secure end.
Weave seam ***(Fig. 15, page 46)***.

Using photo as a guide for Placement, add Appliqués; and Pom-Pom ***(Figs. 16a-c, page 46)***.

Design by Pat Lawrence.

11. LACY CARDIGAN

Size:	Small	Medium	Large
Chest Measurement:	32-34"	36-38"	40-42"
Finished Chest Measurement:	43"	46"	49½"

Size Note: Instructions are written for size Small, with sizes Medium and Large in braces { }. Instructions will be easier to read if you circle all the numbers pertaining to your size. If only one number is given, it applies to all sizes.

MATERIALS

Worsted Weight Yarn:
21 ½ {24-26} ounces,
[610{680-740} grams, 1,350{1,510-1,635} yards]
Straight knitting needles, sizes 6 (4 mm) **and** 7 (4.5 mm)
or sizes needed for gauge
24" Circular needles, sizes 6 (4 mm) **and** 7 (4.5 mm)
or sizes needed for gauge
7/8" Buttons - 6{6-7}
Yarn needle

GAUGE: With large size needles, in pattern,
20 sts and 26 rows = 4"

Note: Cardigan is worked in one piece to underarm.

BODY

RIBBING

With small size circular needle, cast on 226{240-254} sts **loosely**.

Row 1: K2, (P5, K2) across.

Row 2 (Right side)**:** P2, (K5, P2) across.

Row 3: K2, (P5, K2) across.

Row 4: P2, ★ K2 tog ***(Fig. 6, page 44)***, YO ***(Fig. 13a, page 45)***, K1, YO, SSK ***(Figs. 10a-c, page 45)***, P2; repeat from ★ across.

Repeat Rows 1-4 until ribbing measures 4", ending by working a **wrong** side row.

Next Row: Knit across decreasing 15{13-11} sts evenly spaced ***(see Decreases, pages 44 & 45)***: 211{227-243} sts.

BODY

Change to large size circular needle.

Row 1 AND ALL WRONG SIDE ROWS: Purl across.

Row 2 (Right side)**:** K6, YO, SSK, K3, K2 tog, YO, ★ K9, YO, SSK, K3, K2 tog, YO; repeat from ★ across to last 6 sts, K6.

Row 4: K2, YO, SSK, K3, YO, SSK, K1, K2 tog, YO, K3, K2 tog, YO, ★ K1, YO, SSK, K3, YO, SSK, K1, K2 tog, YO, K3, K2 tog, YO; repeat from ★ across to last 2 sts, K2.

Row 6: K3, ★ YO, SSK, K3, YO, [slip 1 as if to **knit**, K2 tog, PSSO ***(Figs. 9a & b, page 44)***], YO, K3, K2 tog, YO, K3; repeat from ★ across.

Row 8: K4, YO, SSK, K7, K2 tog, YO, ★ K5, YO, SSK, K7, K2 tog, YO; repeat from ★ across to last 4 sts, K4.

Row 10: K3, ★ K2 tog, YO, K9, YO, SSK, K3; repeat from ★ across.

Row 12: K2, K2 tog, YO, K3, K2 tog, YO, K1, YO, SSK, K3, YO, SSK, ★ K1, K2 tog, YO, K3, K2 tog, YO, K1, YO, SSK, K3, YO, SSK; repeat from ★ across to last 2 sts, K2.

Row 14: K1, (K2 tog, YO, K3) twice, YO, SSK, K3, YO, ★ slip 1 as if to **knit**, K2 tog, PSSO, YO, K3, K2 tog, YO, K3, YO, SSK, K3, YO; repeat from ★ across to last 3 sts, SSK, K1.

Row 16: K5, K2 tog, YO, K5, YO, SSK, ★ K7, K2 tog, YO, K5, YO, SSK; repeat from ★ across to last 5 sts, K5.

Repeat Rows 1-16 until piece measures approximately 18" from cast on edge, ending by working a **purl** row.

RIGHT FRONT

Note: Maintain established pattern throughout.

Row 1: With large size straight needles, work across 52{56-60} sts; leave remaining 159{171-183} sts on circular needle: 52{56-60} sts.

Work even until Armhole measures approximately 6½{7-7½}", ending by working a **purl** row.

NECK SHAPING

Row 1: Bind off 12{13-14} sts, work across: 40{43-46} sts.

Row 2: Purl across.

Row 3: Bind off 2 sts, work across: 38{41-44} sts.

Rows 4-11: Repeat Rows 2 and 3, 4 times: 30{33-36} sts.

SHOULDER SHAPING

Row 1: Bind off 10{11-12} sts, purl across: 20{22-24} sts.

Row 2: Work across.

Rows 3 and 4: Repeat Rows 1 and 2: 10{11-12} sts.

Bind off remaining sts.

Continued on page 14.

BACK

Note: Maintain established pattern throughout.

Row 1: With **right** side facing and using large size straight needles, work across next 107{115-123} sts, leave remaining 52{56-60} sts on circular needle.

Work even until Armholes measure same as Right Front to Shoulder Shaping, ending by working a **purl** row.

NECK & SHOULDER SHAPING

Note: Both sides of Neck are worked at the same time, using separate yarn for **each** side.

Row 1: Bind off 10{11-12} sts, work across next 29{31-33} sts; with second yarn, bind off next 27{29-31} sts, work across.

Rows 2-4: Bind off 10{11-12} sts, work across; with second yarn, bind off 5 sts, work across.

Row 5: Bind off 10{11-12} sts; with second yarn, bind off 5 sts, work across.

Bind off remaining sts.

LEFT FRONT

Note: Maintain established pattern throughout.

Row 1: With **right** side facing and using large size straight needles, work across remaining 52{56-60} sts.

Work even until Armhole measures same as Right Front to Neck Shaping, ending by working a **right** side row.

NECK SHAPING

Row 1: Bind off 12{13-14} sts, purl across: 40{43-46} sts.

Row 2: Work across.

Row 3: Bind off 2 sts, purl across: 38{41-43} sts.

Rows 4-11: Repeat Rows 2 and 3, 4 times: 30{33-36} sts.

SHOULDER SHAPING

Row 1: Bind off 10{11-12} sts, work across: 20{22-24} sts.

Row 2: Purl across.

Rows 3 and 4: Repeat Rows 1 and 2: 10{11-12} sts.

Bind off remaining sts.

SLEEVE (Make 2)

RIBBING

With small size needles, cast on 51{51-58} sts **loosely**.

Row 1: K2, (P5, K2) across.

Row 2 (Right side)**:** P2, (K5, P2) across.

Row 3: K2, (P5, K2) across.

Row 4: P2, ★ K2 tog, YO, K1, YO, SSK, P2; repeat from ★ across.

Repeat Rows 1-4 until ribbing measures 4", ending by working a **wrong** side row.

Next Row: Knit across decreasing 3{0-2} sts evenly spaced ***(see Zeros, page 43)***: 48{51-56} sts.

BODY

Change to large size needles.

Row 1: Purl across.

Row 2 (Right side)**:** Knit across.

Row 3: Purl across.

Row 4 (Increase row)**:** K1, increase ***(Figs. 3a & b, page 43)***, knit across to last 2 sts, increase, K1: 50{53-58} sts.

Working in Stockinette Stitch, continue to increase one stitch at **each** edge in same manner, every fourth row, 16{17-17} times **more**: 82{87-92} sts.

Work even until Sleeve measures approximately 16½ {17-17}" from cast on edge.

Bind off all sts **loosely**.

FINISHING

Sew shoulder seams.

NECK RIBBING

With **right** side facing, using small size circular needle and beginning at Right Front Neck edge, pick up 121{128-135} sts evenly spaced around Neck edge ***(Figs. 14a & b, page 46)***.

Row 1: K2, (P5, K2) across.

Row 2 (Right side)**:** P2, (K5, P2) across.

Row 3: K2, (P5, K2) across.

Row 4: P2, ★ K2 tog, YO, K1, YO, SSK, P2; repeat from ★ across.

Rows 5-9: Repeat Rows 1-4 once, then repeat Row 1 once **more**.

Bind off all sts **loosely** in pattern.

LEFT FRONT BAND

With **right** side facing, using small size circular needle and working along Neck Ribbing and Left Front edge, pick up 142{149-156} sts evenly spaced across.

Row 1: K2, (P5, K2) across.

Row 2 (Right side): P2, ★ K2 tog, YO, K1, YO, SSK, P2; repeat from ★ across.

Row 3: K2, (P5, K2) across.

Row 4: P2, (K5, P2) across.

Rows 5-8: Repeat Rows 1-4.

Bind off all sts in pattern.

RIGHT FRONT BAND

With **right** side facing, using small size circular needle and working along Right Front edge and Neck Ribbing, pick up 142{149-156} sts evenly spaced across.

Row 1: K2, (P5, K2) across.

Row 2 (Right side)**:** P2,★ K2 tog, YO, K1, YO, SSK, P2; repeat from ★ across.

Row 3: K2, (P5, K2) across.

FOR SIZE SMALL ONLY

Row 4 (Buttonhole row)**:** P2, K1, bind off next 3 sts, (P2, K5) 3 times, P1, bind off next 3 sts, K2, P2, (K5, P2) twice, K4, bind off next 3 sts, K4, P2, (K5, P2) twice, K3, bind off next 3 sts, (K5, P2) 3 times, K2, bind off next 3 sts, P1, (K5, P2) 3 times, K1, bind off next 3 sts, P2: 124 sts.

Row 5: K2, P1, add on 3 sts ***(Figs. 5a & b, page 43)***, **turn**; P1, K2, (P5, K2) 3 times, add on 3 sts, **turn**; P2, (K2, P5) 3 times, K1, add on 3 sts, **turn**; P3, (K2, P5) 3 times, add on 3 sts, **turn**; P4, K2, (P5, K2) twice, P3, add on 3 sts, **turn**; K1, (P5, K2) 3 times, P1, add on 3 sts, **turn**; P1, K2: 142 sts.

Rows 6 and 7: Repeat Rows 2 and 3.

Row 8: P2, (K5, P2) across.

Bind off all sts in pattern.

FOR SIZE MEDIUM ONLY

Row 4 (Buttonhole row)**:** P2, K1, bind off next 3 sts, P2, ★ (K5, P2) 3 times, K1, bind off next 3 sts, P2; repeat from ★ across: 131 sts.

Row 5: K2, P1, add on 3 sts ***(Figs. 5a & b, page 43)***, **turn**; P1, K2, ★ (P5, K2) 3 times, P1, add on 3 sts, **turn**; P1, K2; repeat from ★ across: 149 sts.

Rows 6 and 7: Repeat Rows 2 and 3.

Row 8: P2, (K5, P2) across.

Bind off all sts in pattern.

FOR SIZE LARGE ONLY

Row 4 (Buttonhole row)**:** P2, K1, bind off next 3 sts, P2, ★ (K5, P2) twice, K4, bind off next 3 sts, K4, P2, (K5, P2) twice, K1, bind off next 3 sts, P2; repeat from ★ across: 135 sts.

Row 5: K2, P1, add on 3 sts ***(Figs. 5a & b, page 43)***, **turn**; P1, ★ (K2, P5) 3 times, add on 3 sts, **turn**; P4, K2, (P5, K2) twice, P1, add on 3 sts, **turn**; P1; repeat from ★ across to last 2 sts, K2: 156 sts.

Rows 6 and 7: Repeat Rows 2 and 3.

Row 8: P2, (K5, P2) across.

Bind off all sts in pattern.

Sew Sleeve seams. Sew Sleeves to Sweater, matching center of last row on Sleeve to shoulder seam.

Sew buttons to Left Front Band.

Design by Deborah Newton.

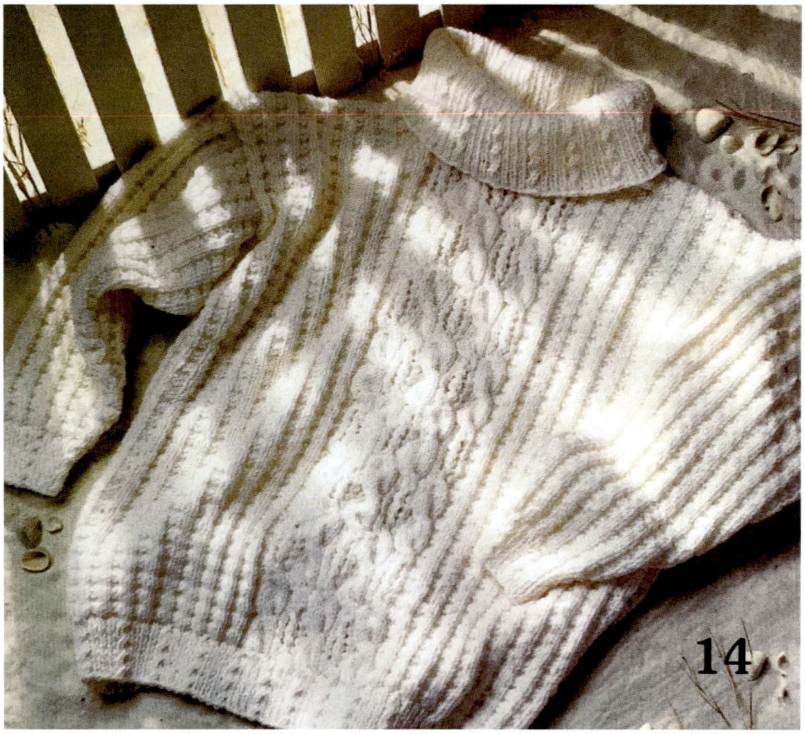
14

2

1
24

22

12. HOODED RAGLAN PULLOVER

Size:	4	6	8	10	12
Chest Measurement:	27"	29"	30½"	32"	34"
Finished Chest Measurement:	24"	25½"	27"	28½"	30"

Size Note: Instructions are written with sizes 4 and 6 in the first set of braces { } and with sizes 8, 10, and 12 in the second set of braces. Instructions will be easier to read if you circle all the numbers pertaining to your size. If only one number is given, it applies to all sizes.

MATERIALS

Worsted Weight Yarn: (4 MEDIUM)
{12-14}{16-17-19} ounces,
[{340-400}{450-480-540} grams,
{780-910}{1, 040-1, 110-1,240} yards]
Straight knitting needles, sizes 5 (3. 75 mm) and 7 (4.5 mm) **or** sizes needed for gauge
Markers
Stitch holders - 5
Yarn needle
Sewing needle and thread
5/8" Button

GAUGE: With large size needles, in Stockinette Stitch, 20 sts and 26 rows = 4"

Note: Row gauge is very important in raglans ***(see Gauge, page 42)***. To correct your row gauge if you have obtained stitch gauge, but have more rows per inch than specified, use a larger needle for the purl rows. If you have fewer rows per inch, use a smaller needle for the purl rows.

BACK

RIBBING

With small size needles, cast on {70-74}{78-82-88} sts **loosely**.

Work in K1, P1 ribbing for {1½-1½}{2-2-2}".

BODY

Change to large size needles.

Work in Stockinette Stitch until Back measures approximately {9-10}{11-11½-12}" from cast on edge or desired length to underarm, ending by working a **purl** row.

RAGLAN SHAPING

Rows 1 and 2: Bind off 4 sts at the beginning of the next 2 rows, work across: {62-66}{70-74-80} sts.

Row 3 (Decrease row)**:** K1, SSK ***(Figs. 10a-c, page 45),*** knit across to last 3 sts, K2 tog ***(Fig. 6, page 44)***, K1: {60-64}{68-72-78} sts.

Continue to decrease one stitch at **each** edge in same manner, every fourth row, {1-2}{2-2-1} time(s) **more;** then decrease every other row, {18-18}{19-21-24} times, ending by working a **right** side row: {22-24}{26-26-28} sts.

Slip remaining sts onto st holder; cut yarn.

FRONT

Work same as Back until {42-48}{50-54-56} sts remain, ending by working a **purl** row.

LEFT PLACKET

For Girls' Only - Row 1 (Decrease row)**:** K1, SSK, knit {14-17}{18-20-21} sts, slip remaining {25-28}{29-31-32} sts onto st holder, add on 8 sts for Garter Stitch Placket ***(Figs. 5a & b, page 43)***: {24-27}{28-30-31} sts.

For Boy's Only - Row 1 (Decrease row)**:** K1, SSK, knit {14-17}{18-20-21} sts, K8 for Garter Stitch Placket, slip remaining {17-20}{21-23-24} sts onto st holder: {24-27}{28-30-31} sts.

Row 2: K8, purl across.

Row 3 (Decrease row)**:** K1, SSK, knit across: {23-26}{27-29-30} sts.

Row 4: K8, purl across.

Repeat Rows 3 and 4, {8-10}{10-12-12} times: {15-16}{17-17-18} sts.

Slip remaining sts onto st holder; cut yarn.

RIGHT PLACKET

For Girls' Only - Row 1 (Decrease row)**:** Slip {25-28}{29-31-32} sts from st holder onto large size needle, K8 for Garter Stitch Placket, place marker ***(see Markers, page 43)***, knit across to last 3 sts, K2 tog, K1: {24-27}{28-30-31} sts.

For Boy's Only - Row 1 (Decrease row)**:** Slip {17-20}{21-23-24} sts from st holder onto large size needle, add on 8 sts for Garter Stitch Placket ***(Figs. 5a & b, page 43)***, K8, place marker ***(see Markers, page 43)***, knit across to last 3 sts, K2 tog, K1: {24-27}{28-30-31} sts.

Row 2: Purl across to marker, K8.

Row 3 (Decrease row)**:** Knit across to last 3 sts, K2 tog, K1: {23-26}{27-29-30} sts.

Row 4: Purl across to marker, K8.

Repeat Rows 3 and 4, {8-10}{10-12-12} times; do **not** cut yarn, slip remaining {15-16}{17-17-18} sts onto st holder.

POUCH

With small size needles, cast on {70-74}{78-82-88) sts **loosely**.

Change to large size needles.

Row 1: Knit across.

Row 2: K6, place marker, purl across to last 6 sts, place marker, K6.

Row 3: Knit across.

Row 4: K6, purl across to marker, K6.

Repeat Rows 3 and 4 until Pouch measures approximately {2-2½}{3-3-3}" from cast on edge, ending by working Row 4.

Note: Loop a short piece of yarn around first and last st on last row.

SHAPING

Row 1 (Decrease row)**:** K6, SSK, knit across to within 2 sts of marker, K2 tog, K6: {68-72}{76-80-86) sts.

Row 2: K6, purl across to marker, K6.

Repeat Rows 1 and 2, {13-13}{14-14-14} times: {42-46}{48-52-58} sts.

Last 10 Rows: Knit across.

Bind off all sts.

Sew Pouch to Front, sewing cast on edge of Pouch just above Ribbing and side edges up to marked row. Sew bound off edge to Front.

SLEEVE (Make 2)

RIBBING

With small size needles, cast on{38-38}{40-40-40} sts **loosely**.

Work in K1, P1 ribbing for approximately {2-2}{2½-2½-2½}" increasing 4 sts evenly spaced across last row ***(see Increases, page 43)***: {42-42}{44-44-44} sts.

BODY

Change to large size needles.

Work in Stockinette Stitch, increasing one stitch at **each** edge, every tenth row, {3-4}{4-6-7} times: {48-50}{52-56-58) sts.

Work even until Sleeve measures approximately {10½-10¾}{13-14¼-15½}" from cast on edge or desired length to underarm, ending by working a **purl** row.

RAGLAN SHAPING

Rows 1 and 2: Bind off 4 sts at the beginning of the next 2 rows, work across: {40-42}{44-48-50} sts.

Row 3 (Decrease row)**:** K1, SSK, knit across to last 3 sts, K2 tog, K1: {38-40}{42-46-48} sts.

Row 4: Purl across.

Row 5: K1, slip 1 as if to **purl**, knit across to last 2 sts, slip 1 as if to **purl**, K1.

Row 6: Purl across.

Row 7 (Decrease row)**:** K1, SSK, knit across to last 3 sts, K2 tog, K1: {36-38}{40-44-46} sts.

Repeat Rows 4-7, {4-5}{5-6-6} times; then repeat Rows 6 and 7, {10-10}{11-11-12} times **more**: {8-8}{8-10-10} sts.

Slip remaining sts onto st holder; cut yarn.

FINISHING

Weave raglan seams ***(Fig. 15, page 46)***.
Weave underarm and side in one continuous seam.

NECK BAND & HOOD

Row 1: Slip sts from right Front st holder onto small size needle and knit across, knit sts from right Sleeve, Back and left Sleeve st holders, slip sts from left Front st holder onto empty needle and knit across: {68-72}{76-80-84} sts.

Rows 2-4: Knit across.

For Girls' Only - Row 5 (Buttonhole row)**:** K3, YO ***(Fig. 13a, page 45)***, K2 tog, knit across.

For Boy's Only - Row 5 (Buttonhole row)**:** Knit across to last 5 sts, K2 tog, YO ***(Fig. 13a, page 45)***, K3.

Rows 6-9: Knit across.

Rows 10 and 11: Bind off 8 sts, K7 for Garter Stitch Border, place marker, knit across: {52-56}{60-64-68} sts.

Change to large size needles.

Row 12: K8, purl across to marker, K8.

Row 13: Knit across increasing {18-20}{22-22-24} sts evenly spaced between markers: {70-76}{82-86-92} sts.

Row 14: K8, purl across to marker, K8.

Row 15: Knit across.

Repeat Rows 14 and 15 until Hood measures approximately {12-13}{13-13-14}" or desired length to top of head.

Bind off all sts; cut yarn leaving an 18" length for sewing.

Fold Hood at center back with **wrong** sides together and sew bound off edge together.
Sew bottom edge of Placket to **wrong** side.
Sew button to Placket opposite buttonhole.

9

17

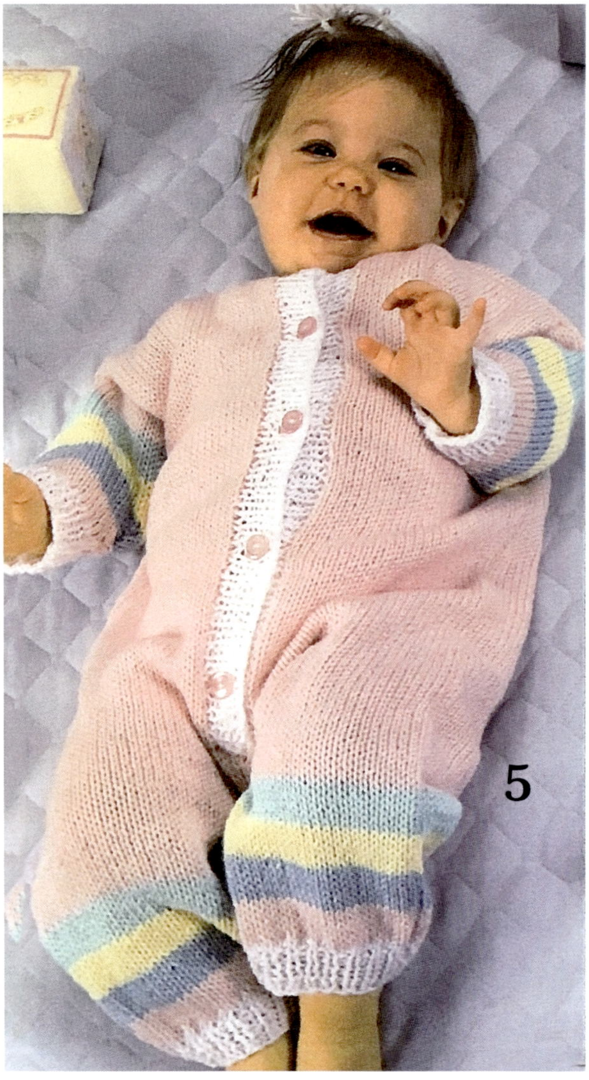

5

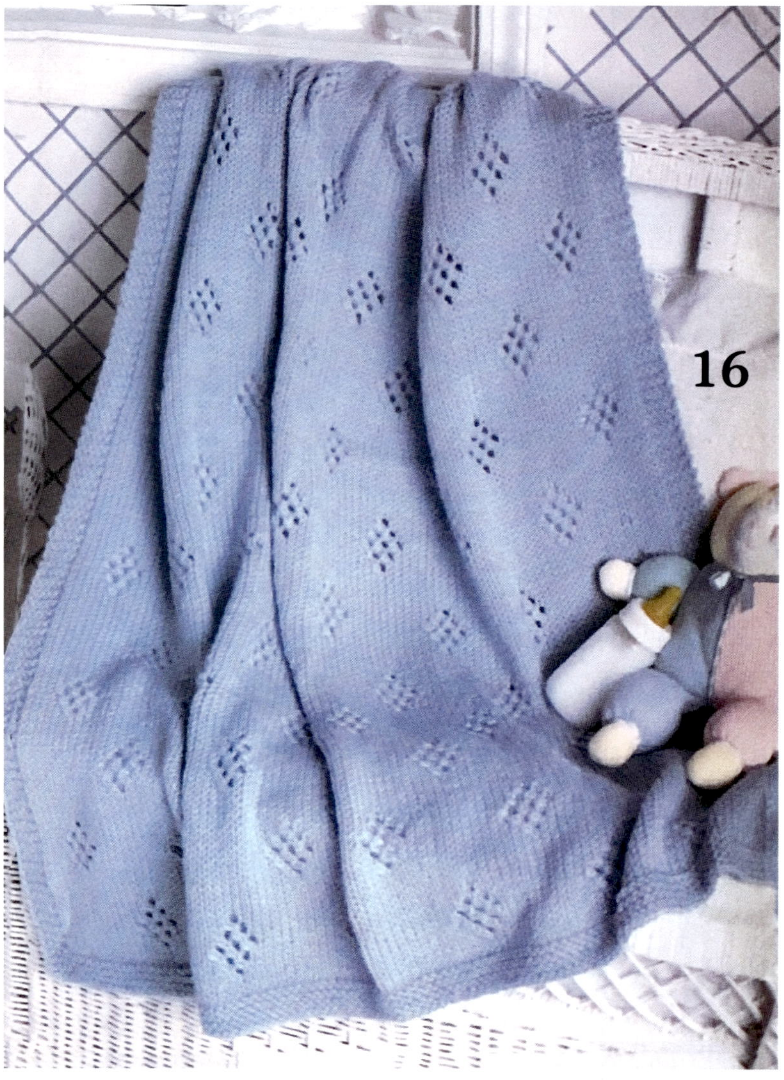

16

18

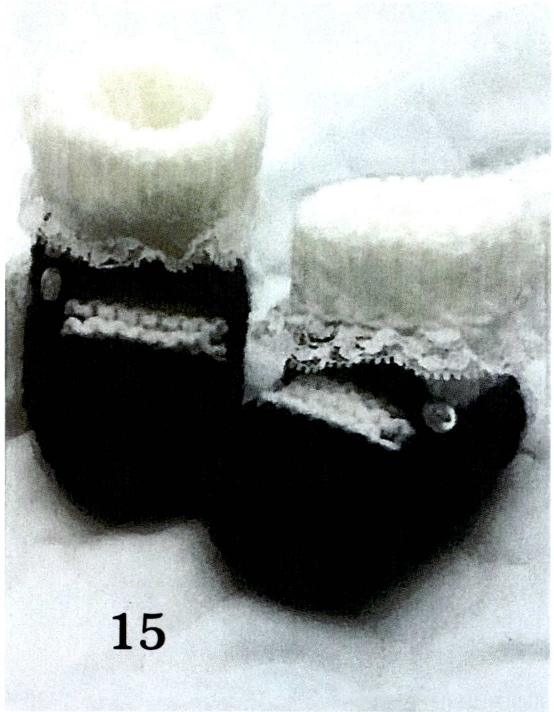
15

19

13. CARDIGAN VEST

Size:	32	34	36	38	40
Chest Measurement:	32"	34"	36"	38"	40"
Finished Chest Measurement:	34"	36"	38"	40"	42"

Size Note: Instructions are written with sizes 32 and 34 in the first set of braces { } and with sizes 36, 38, and 40 in the second set of braces. Instructions will be easier to read if you circle all the numbers pertaining to your size. If only one number is given, it applies to all sizes.

MATERIALS

Worsted Weight Yarn: MEDIUM 4
- Red- {8½-9}{9½-10-10½} ounces, **[**{240-260}{270-280-300} grams, {530-560}{590-625-655} yards**]**
- White - {3½-3½}{4-4-4} ounces, **[**{100-100}{110-110-110} grams, {220-220}{250-250-250} yards**]**

Straight knitting needles, sizes 5 (3. 75 mm) **and** 7 (4.5 mm) **or** sizes needed for gauge
Stitch holders - 3
Yarn needle
¼" Buttons - 7

GAUGE: With large size needles,
in Stockinette Stitch, 20 sts and 26 rows = 4"

BACK

RIBBING

With small size needles and Red, cast on {80-84}{88-92-100} sts **loosely**.

Work in K2, P2 ribbing for 2" increasing {8-8}{10-10-8} sts evenly spaced across last row ***(see Increases, page 43)***: {88-92}{98-102-108} sts.

BODY

Change to large size needles.

Work in Garter Stitch until Right Front measures approximately 9½" from cast on edge, ending by working a **purl** row.

ARMHOLE SHAPING

Rows 1 and 2: Bind off 2 sts at the beginning of the next 2 rows, work across: {84-88}{94-98-104} sts.

Row 3 (Decrease row)**:** Slip 1 as if to **knit**, K1, PSSO ***(Figs. 8a & b, page 44)***, knit across to last 2 sts, K2 tog ***(Fig. 6, page 44)***: {82-86}{92-96-102} sts.

Row 4: Purl across.

Rows 5-8: Repeat Rows 3 and 4 twice: {78-82}{88-92-98} sts.

Work even until Armholes measure approximately 10½", ending by working a **knit** row.

NECK SHAPING

Note: Both sides of Neck are worked at the same time, using separate yarn for **each** side.

Row 1: Purl {26-28}{30-31-33} sts, slip next {26-26}{28-30-32} sts onto st holder; with second yarn, purl across: {26-28}{30-31-33} sts **each** side.

Row 2 (Decrease row)**:** Knit across to within 2 sts Neck edge, K2 tog; with second yarn, slip 1 as if to **knit**, K1, PSSO, knit across: {25-27}{29-30-32} sts **each** side.

Row 3: Purl across; with second yarn, purl across.

Rows 4-7: Repeat Rows 2 and 3 twice: {23-25}{27-28-30} sts **each** side.

Bind off remaining sts.

RIGHT FRONT

RIBBING

With small size needles and White, cast on {40-40}{44-48-48} sts **loosely**.

Work in K2, P2 ribbing for 2" increasing {2-4}{4-2-4} sts evenly spaced across last row: {42-44}{48-50-52} sts.

BODY

Change to large size needles.

Work Garter Stitch until Right Front measures approximately 9½" from cast on edge.

ARMHOLE SHAPING

Row 1 (Wrong side)**:** Bind off 2 sts, knit across: {40-42}{46-48-50} sts.

Row 2 (Decrease row)**:** Knit across to last 2 sts, K2 tog: {39-41}{45-47-49} sts.

Row 3: Knit across.

Rows 4-7: Repeat Rows 2 and 3 twice: {37-39}{43-45-47} sts.

Cut White; with Red and beginning with a **knit** row, work in Stockinette Stitch until Armhole measures approximately 9½", ending by working a **knit** row.

NECK SHAPING

Row 1: Purl {26-28}{30-31-33} sts, slip remaining {11-11}{13-14-14} sts onto st holder.

Row 2 (Decrease row)**:** Slip 1 as if to **knit**, K1, PSSO, knit across: {25-27}{29-30-32} sts.

Row 3: Purl across.

Rows 4-7: Repeat Rows 2 and 3 twice: {23-25}{27-28-30} sts.

Work even until Armhole measures same as Back, ending by working a **purl** row.

Bind off remaining sts.

LEFT FRONT

RIBBING

With Red, work same as Right Front.

BODY

Change to large size needles.

Work in Stockinette Stitch until Left Front measures same as Right Front to Armhole Shaping, ending by working a **purl** row.

ARMHOLE SHAPING

Row 1: Bind off 2 sts, knit across: {40-42}{46-48-50} sts.

Row 2: Purl across.

Row 3 (Decrease row)**:** Slip 1 as if to **knit**, K1, PSSO, knit across: {39-41}{45-47-49} sts.

Rows 4-7: Repeat Rows 2 and 3 twice: {37-39}{43-45-47} sts.

Row 8: Purl across.

Cut Red; with White, work in Garter Stitch until Armhole measures same as Right Front to Neck Shaping, ending by working a **wrong** side row.

NECK SHAPING

Row 1: Knit {26-28}{30-31-33} sts, slip remaining {11-11}{13-14-14} sts onto st holder.

Row 2: Knit across.

Row 3 (Decrease row)**:** Knit across to last 2 sts, K2 tog: {25-27}{29-30-32} sts.

Rows 4-7: Repeat Rows 2 and 3 twice: {23-25}{27-28-30} sts.

Work even until Armhole measures same as Back, ending by working a **wrong** side row.

Bind off remaining sts.

FINISHING

RIGHT FRONT BAND

With **right** side facing, using small size needles and Red, pick up 96 sts evenly spaced across Right Front edge ***(Fig. 14a, page 46)***.

Rows 1 and 2: (K2, P2) across.

Row 3 (Buttonhole row)**:** Work across 8 sts, bind off next 2 sts, ★ work across 13 sts, bind off next 2 sts; repeat from ★ 4 times **more**, work across 5 sts: 84 sts.

Row 4: ★ Work across to bound off sts, add on 2 sts ***(Figs. 5a & b, page 43)***, **turn**; repeat from ★ 5 times **more**, work across: 96 sts.

Rows 5-7: (K2, P2) across.

Bind off all sts **tightly** in ribbing.

LEFT FRONT BAND

With **right** side facing. using small size needles and Red, pick up 96 sts evenly spaced across Left Front edge.

Work in K2, P2 ribbing for 7 rows.

Bind off all sts **tightly** in ribbing.

Sew shoulder seams.

NECK RIBBING

With **right** side facing, using small size needles and Red, pick up 6 sts along end of Right Front Band, knit {11-11}{13-14-14} sts from Right Front st holder, pick up {13-13}{12-12-13} sts along Right Neck edge, knit {26-26}{28-30-32} sts from Back st holder, pick up {13-13}{12-12-13} sts along Left Neck edge, slip {11-11}{13-14-14} sts from Left Front st holder onto empty needle and knit across, pick up 6 sts along end of Left Front Band: {86-86}{90-94-98} sts.

Row 1: P2, (K2, P2) across.

Row 2: K2, (P2, K2) across.

Row 3 (Buttonhole row)**:** P2, (K2, P2) across to last 4 sts, bind off next 2 sts, P1.

Row 4: K2, add on 2 sts, **turn**; K2, (P2, K2) across.

Rows 5-7: Repeat Rows 1 and 2 once, then repeat Row 1 once **more**.

Bind off all sts **loosely** in ribbing.

ARMHOLE RIBBING

With **right** side facing, using small size needles and Red, pick up 96 sts evenly spaced across.

Work in K2, P2 ribbing for 1".

Bind off all sts **loosely** in ribbing.

Repeat for second Armhole.

Weave side seams ***(Fig. 15, page 46)***.
Sew buttons to Left Front.

Design by Linda J. Martin.

10

12

13

23

3
FORE

4

21
20
OPEC moves

14. TURTLENECK PULLOVER

Size:	**Small**	**Medium**	**Large**
Chest Measurement:	32-34"	36-38"	40-42"
Finished Chest Measurement:	40½"	45½"	50"

Size Note: Instructions are written for size Small, with sizes Medium and Large in braces { }. Instructions will be easier to read if you circle all the numbers pertaining to your size. If only one number is given, it applies to all sizes.

MATERIALS

Worsted Weight Yarn:
23(25½-28} ounces,
[650{720-800) grams, 1,445{1,605-1,760) yards]
Straight knitting needles, sizes 6 (4 mm) and 7 (4.5 mm)
or sizes needed for gauge
16" Circular needle, size 7 (4.5 mm)
Cable needle
Markers
Yarn needle

GAUGE: With large size needles,
in Back Body pattern, 20 sts and 28 rows = 4"

STITCH GUIDE

TWIST
K2 tog ***(Fig. 6, page 44)*** but do **not** slip sts off the left needle, knit first st again, slipping both sts off the left needle.

CABLE (use 6 sts)
Slip next 3 st onto cable needle and hold in front of work, K3 from left needle, K3 from cable needle.

FRONT CROSS *(abbreviated FC)* (use next 2 sts)
Slip 1 as if to **purl** onto cable needle and hold in **front** of work, K1 from left needle, K1 from cable needle.

BACK

RIBBING

With small size needle, cast on 107{120-129} sts **loosely**.

Row 1: K1, (P1, K1) 1{2-2} time(s), P2, ★ K1, (P1, K1) 3 times, P2; repeat from ★ across to last 3{5-5} sts, K1, (P1, K1) 1{2-2} time(s).

Row 2 (Right side): P1, (K1, P1) 1{2-2} time(s), work Twist, ★ P1, (K1, P1) 3 times, work Twist; repeat from ★ across to last 3{5-5} sts, P1, (K1, P1) 1{2-2} time(s).

Row 3: K1, (P1, K1) 1{2-2} time(s), P2, ★ K1, (P1, K1) 3 times, P2; repeat from ★ across to last 3 {5-5} sts, K1, (P1, K1) 1{2-2} time(s).

Row 4: P1, (K1, P1) 1{2-2} time(s), K2, ★ P1, (K1, P1) 3 times, K2; repeat from ★ across to last 3 {5-5} sts, P1, (K1, P1) 1{2-2} time(s).

Repeat Rows 1-4 until ribbing measures 2½", ending by working a **right** side row.

BODY

Row 1: Purl across decreasing 3{4-1} st(s) evenly spaced ***(see Decreases, pages 44 & 45 and Fig. 11, page 45)***: 104 {116-128 sts} sts.

Change to large size needles.

Row 2 (Right side): Knit across.

Row 3: P1, K2, (P2, K2) across to last st, P1.

Row 4: K1, P2, (K2, P2), across to last st, K1.

Row 5: Purl across.

Repeat Rows 2-5 for pattern until Back measures approximately 26½"{27-27½}" from cast on edge, ending by working a **wrong** side row.

NECK & SHOULDER SHAPING

Note: Both sides of Neck are worked at the same time, using separate yarn for **each** side. Maintain established pattern throughout.

Row 1: Bind off 11 {13-14} sts, work across 31{34-38} sts; with second yarn, bind off next 18{20-22} sts, work across.

Row 2-4: Bind off 11{13-14} sts, work across; with second yarn, bind off 5 sts, work across.

Row 5: Bind off 11{12-15} sts; with second yarn, bind off 5 sts, work across.

Bind off remaining sts.

FRONT

RIBBING

Work same as Back.

BODY

Row 1: Purl across increasing 1{0-1} st(s) ***(see Zeros, page 43)*** at end of row ***(Fig. 4, page 43)***: 108{120-130} sts.

Change to large size needles.

Row 2 (Right side): K 36{42-47}, place marker ***(see Markers, page 43)***, P1, work Cable, P1, ★ K6, P1, work Cable, P1; repeat from ★ once **more**, place marker, knit across.

Row 3: P2{0-1}, K2, (P2, K2) across to marker, K1, (P6, K1) across to next marker, K2, (P2, K2) across to last 2{0-1} st(s), P2{0-1}.

Row 4: K2{0-1}, P2, (K2, P2) across to marker, P1, K6, P1, ★ work Cable, P1, K6, P1; repeat from ★ once **more**, P2, (K2, P2) across to last 2{0-1} st(s), K2{0-1}.

Row 5: Purl across to marker, K1, (P6, K1) across to next marker, purl across.

Note: When instructed to slip a stitch, always slip as if to **knit**, unless otherwise instructed.

Row 6: Knit across to marker, P1, K6, P1, ★ slip 1, K1, PSSO ***(Figs. 8a & b, page 44)***, YO ***(Fig. 13a, page 45)***, K2, YO, K2 tog ***(Fig. 6, page 44)***, P1, K6, P1; repeat from ★ once **more**, knit across.

Row 7: P2{0-1}, K2, (P2, K2) across to marker, K1, (P6, K1) across to next marker, K2, (P2, K2) across to last 2{0-1} st(s), P2{0-1}.

Row 8: K2{0-1}, P2, (K2, P2) across to marker, P1, K6, P1, ★ slip 1, K1, PSSO, YO, work FC, YO, K2 tog, P1, K6, P1; repeat from ★ once **more**, P2, (K2, P2) across to last 2{0-1} st(s), K2{0-1}.

Row 9: Purl across to marker, K1, (P6, K1) across to next marker, purl across.

Row 10: Knit across to marker, P1, K6, P1, ★ slip 1, K1, PSSO, YO, K2, YO, K2 tog, P1, K6, P1; repeat from ★ once **more**, knit across.

Row 11: P2{0-1}, K2, (P2, K2) across to marker, K1, (P6, K1) across to next marker, K2, (P2, K2) across to last 2{0-1} st(s), P2{0-1}.

Row 12: K2{0-1}, P2, (K2, P2) across to marker, P1, work Cable, P1, ★ slip 1, K1, PSSO, YO, work FC, YO, K2 tog, P1, work Cable, P1; repeat from ★ once **more**, P2, (K2, P2) across to last 2{0-1} st(s), K2{0-1}.

Row 13: Purl across to marker, K1, (P6, K1) across to next marker, purl across.

Row 14: Knit across to marker, P1, K6, P1, ★ slip 1, K1, PSSO, YO, K2, YO, K2 tog, P1, K6, P1; repeat from ★ once **more**, knit across.

Row 15: P2{0-1}, K2, (P2, K2) across to marker, K1, (P6, K1) across to next marker, K2, (P2, K2) across to last 2{0-1} st(s), P2{0-1}.

Row 16: K2{0-1}, P2, (K2, P2) across to marker, P1, K6, P1, ★ slip 1, K1, PSSO, YO, work FC, YO, K2 tog, P1, K6, P1; repeat from ★ once **more**, P2, (K2, P2) across to last 2{0-1} st(s), K2{0-1}.

Row 17: Purl across to marker, K1, (P6, K1) across to next marker; purl across.

Row 18: Knit across to marker, P1, (K6, P1) across to next marker, knit across.

Row 19: P2{0-1}, K2, (P2, K2) across to marker, K1, (P6, K1) across to next marker, K2, (P2, K2) across to last 2{0-1} st(s), P2{0-1}.

Row 20: K2{0-1}, P2, (K2, P2) across to marker, P1, K6, P1, ★ work Cable, P1, K6, P1; repeat from ★ once **more**, P2, (K2, P2) across to last 2{0-1} st(s), K2{0-1}.

Row 21: Purl across to marker, K1, (P6, K1) across to next marker, purl across.

Row 22: Knit across to marker, P1, work Cable, P1,★ K6, P1, work Cable, P1; repeat from ★ once **more**, knit across.

Row 23: P2{0-1}, K2, (P2, K2) across to marker, K1, (P6, K1) across to next marker, K2, (P2, K2) across to last 2{0-1} st(s), P2{0-1}.

Row 24: K2{0-1}, P2, (K2, P2) across to marker, P1, slip 1, K1, PSSO, YO, K2, YO, K2 tog, P1, ★ K6, P1, slip 1, K1, PSSO, YO, K2, YO, K2 tog, P1; repeat from ★ once **more**, P2, (K2, P2) across to last 2{0-1} st(s), K2{0-1}.

Row 25: Purl across to marker, K1, (P6, K1) across to next marker, purl across.

Row 26: Knit across to marker, P1, slip 1, K1, PSSO, YO, work FC, YO, K2 tog, P1, ★ K6, P1, slip 1, K1, PSSO, YO, work FC, YO, K2 tog, P1; repeat from ★ once **more**, knit across.

Row 27: P2{0-1}, K2, (P2, K2) across to marker, K1, (P6, K1) across to next marker, K2, (P2, K2) across to last 2{0-1} st(s), P2{0-1}.

Row 28: K2{0-1}, P2, (K2, P2) across to marker, P1, slip 1, K1, PSSO, YO, K2, YO, K2 tog, P1, ★ K6, P1, slip 1, K1, PSSO, YO, K2, YO, K2 tog, P1, repeat from ★ once **more**, P2, (K2, P2) across to last 2{0-1} st(s), K2{0-1}.

Row 29: Purl across to marker, K1, (P6, K1) across to next marker, purl across.

Row 30: Knit across to marker, P1, slip 1, K1, PSSO, YO, work FC, YO, K2 tog, P1, ★ work Cable, P1, slip 1, K1, PSSO, YO, work FC, YO, K2 tog, P1; repeat from ★ once **more**, knit across.

Row 31: P2{0-1}, K2, (P2, K2) across to marker, K1, (P6, K1) across to next marker, K2, (P2, K2) across to last 2{0-1} st(s), P2{0-1}.

Row 32: K2{0-1}, P2, (K2, P2) across to marker, P1, slip 1, K1, PSSO, YO, K2, YO, K2 tog, P1, ★ K6, P1, slip 1, K1, PSSO, YO, K2, YO, K2 tog, P1; repeat from ★ once **more**, P2, (K2, P2) across to last 2{0-1} st(s), K2{0-1}.

Row 33: Purl across to marker, K1, (P6, K1) across to next marker, purl across.

Row 34: Knit across to marker, P1, slip 1, K1, PSSO, YO, work FC, YO, K2 tog, P1, ★ K6, P1, slip 1, K1, PSSO, YO, work FC, YO, K2 tog, P1; repeat from ★ once **more**, knit across.

Row 35: P2{0-1}, K2, (P2, K2) across to marker, K1, (P6, K1) across to next marker, K2, (P2, K2) across to last 2{0-1} st(s), P2{0-1}.

Row 36: K2{0-1}, P2, (K2, P2) across to marker, P1, (K6, P1) across to next marker, P2, (K2, P2) across to last 2{0-1} st(s), K2{0-1}.

Row 37: Purl across to marker, K1, (P6, K1) across to next marker, purl across.

Row 38: Knit across to marker, P1, work Cable, P1, ★ K6, P1, work Cable, P1; repeat from ★ once **more**, knit across.

Repeat Rows 3-38 for pattern until Front measures approximately 24½{25-25½}" from cast on edge, ending by working a **wrong** side row.

NECK SHAPING

Note: Both sides of Neck are worked at the same time, using separate yarn for **each** side. Maintain established pattern throughout.

Row 1: Work across 43{48-53} sts; with second yarn, bind off next 22{24-24) sts, work across: 43{48-53} sts **each** side.

Rows 2-11: Work across; with second yarn, bind off 2 sts, work across: 33{38-43} sts **each** side.

Work even until Front measures same as Back to Shoulder Shaping, ending by working a **wrong** side row.

SHOULDER SHAPING

Rows 1-4: Bind off 11{13-14} sts, work across; with second yarn, work across: 11{12-15} sts **each** side.

Row 5: Bind off 11{12-15} sts; with second yarn, work across

Bind off remaining sts.

SLEEVE (Make 2)

RIBBING

With small size needles, cast on 44{44-48} sts **loosely**.

Work same as Back.

BODY

Row 1: Purl across increasing 2{6-2) sts evenly spaced ***(see Increases, page 43)***: 46{50-50} sts.

Change to large size needles.

Row 2 (Right side)**:** Knit across.

Row 3: K2, (P2, K2) across.

Row 4 (Increase row)**:** P1, increase, K2, (P2, K2) across to last 2 sts, increase, P1: 48{52-52} sts.

Row 5: Purl across.

Row 6: Knit across.

Row 7: P1, K2, (P2, K2) across to last st, P1.

Row 8 (Increase row)**:** K1, increase, P1, K2, (P2, K2) across to last 3 sts, P1, increase, K1: 50{54-54} sts.

Maintaining pattern, continue to increase one stitch at **each** edge in same manner, every fourth row, 18{19-22} times **more**: 86{92-98} sts.

Work even until Sleeve measures approximately 16½{17-17½}" from cast on edge.

Bind off all sts **loosely**.

FINISHING

Sew shoulder seams.

NECK RIBBING

With **right** side facing, beginning at right shoulder seam and using circular needle, pick up 135{144-153} sts evenly spaced around Neck edge **(*Figs. 14a & b, page 46*)**, place marker to mark beginning of rnd.

Note: Turn work so **wrong** side of neckline (inside) is facing and so the last stitch picked up will be the first stitch worked.

Rnd 1: ★ P1, (K1, P1) 3 times, K2; repeat from ★ around.

Rnd 2: ★ P1, (K1, P1) 3 times, work Twist; repeat from ★ around.

Rnds 3-5: ★ P1 (K1, P1) 3 times, K2; repeat from ★ around.

Repeat Rnds 2-5 until ribbing measure 6".

Bind off all sts **loosely** in pattern.

Sew Sleeves to sweater, matching center of last row on Sleeve to shoulder seam and beginning 8½ {9-9½}" down from seam.

Wave underarm and side in one continuous seam ***(Fig. 15, page 46)***.

Design by Deborah Newton.

15. MARY JANE BOOTIES

Finished Size: Newborn

MATERIALS

Sport Weight Yarn: LIGHT 3
- Black - ½ ounce (20 grams 50 yards}
- White - ½ ounce (20 grams, 50 yards)

Straight knitting needles, size 4 (3.5 mm) **or** size needed for gauge
Yarn needle
Sewing needle and thread
½" Gathered lace edging - ½ yard
3/8" Buttons - 2

GAUGE: In Garter Stitch, 11 sts and 20 rows = 2"

BOOTIE

SOLE

With Black, cast on 4 sts **loosely**.

Row 1: Knit across.

Row 2: K1, increase twice ***(Figs. 3a & b, page 43)***, K1: 6 sts.

Row 3: Knit across.

Row 4: K2, increase, K3: 7 sts.

Rows 5-12: Knit across.

Row 13: K3, increase, K3: 8 sts.

Row 14: Knit across.

Row 15: K3, increase, K4: 9 sts.

Row 16: Knit across.

Row 17: K4, increase, K4: 10 sts.

Work in Garter Stitch until Sole measures approximately 3" from cast on edge.

Next Row: K1, K2 tog ***(Fig. 6, page 44)***, K4, K2 tog, K1: 8 sts.

Last Row: K1, K2 tog, K2, K2 tog, K1: 6 sts.

Bind off all sts **loosely**.

SIDES

With Black, cast on 42 sts **loosely**.

Rows 1-8: Knit across.

Note: Begin working in short rows.

Row 9 (Right side)**:** K 24, K2 tog, leave remaining 16 sts unworked; turn.

Rows 10-14: K7, K2 tog, leave remaining sts unworked; turn.

Cut yarn.

Rows 15-19: With White, K7, K2 tog, leave remaining sts unworked; turn.

Row 20: K7, K2 tog, P 11: 30 sts.

Row 21: Knit across.

CUFF

Work in K1, P1 ribbing for 2½ ".

Bind off all sts **loosely** in ribbing.

STRAP

With Black, cast on 12 sts **loosely**.

Bind off all sts **loosely** in knit.

FINISHING

Sew back seam.
Sew Sole to Sides.
Sew a 9" length of lace to Cuff, stretching Cuff as needed; fold Cuff down.

Using photo as a guide for placement, tack Strap in place and sew on button.

Design by Cindy Bracken.

---

16. DIAMONDS BABY AFGHAN

Finished Size: 33" x 44"

MATERIALS

Worsted Weight Yarn: MEDIUM 4
- 19 ounces, (540 grams, 1,110 yards)

29" Circular needles, sizes 9 (5.5 mm) **and** 10 (6 mm) **or** sizes needed for gauge

GAUGE: With large size needles, in Stockinette Stitch, 16 sts and 20 rows = 4"

AFGHAN

With small size needles, cast on 134 sts.

Rows 1-7: Knit across.

Change to large size needles.

Row 8 (Right side)**:** Knit across.

Row 9: K5, purl across to last 5 sts, K5.

Rows 10 and 11: Repeat Rows 8 and 9.

Row 12: K 18, YO ***(Fig. 13a, page 45)***, SSK ***(Figs. 10a-c, page 45)***, ★ K 14, YO, SSK; repeat from ★ across to last 18 sts, K 18.

Continued on page 30.

Row 13: K5, purl across to last 5 sts, K5.

Row 14: K 17, (YO, SSK) twice, ★ K 12, (YO, SSK) twice; repeat from ★ across to last 17 sts, K 17.

Row 15: K5, purl across to last 5 sts, K5.

Row 16: K 16, (YO, SSK) 3 times, ★ K 10, (YO, SSK) 3 times; repeat from ★ across to last 16 sts, K 16.

Row 17: K5, purl across to last 5 sts, K5.

Row 18: K 17, (YO, SSK) twice, ★ K 12, (YO, SSK) twice; repeat from ★ across to last 17 sts, K 17.

Row 19: K5, purl across to last 5 sts, K5.

Row 20: K 18, YO, SSK, ★ K 14, YO, SSK; repeat from ★ across to last 18 sts, K 18.

Row 21: K5, purl across to last 5 sts, K5.

Row 22: Knit across.

Rows 23-25: Repeat Rows 21 and 22 once, then repeat Row 21 once **more**.

Row 26: K 10, YO, SSK, ★ K 14, YO, SSK; repeat from ★ across to last 10 sts, K 10.

Row 27: K5, purl across to last 5 sts, K5.

Row 28: K9, (YO, SSK) twice,★ K 12, (YO, SSK) twice; repeat from ★ across to last 9 sts, K9.

Row 29: K5, purl across to last 5 sts, K5.

Row 30: K8, (YO, SSK) 3 times, ★ K 10, (YO, SSK) 3 times; repeat from ★ across to last 8 sts, K8.

Row 31: K5, purl across to last 5 sts, K5.

Row 32: K9, (YO, SSK) twice, ★ K 12, (YO, SSK) twice; repeat from ★ across to last 9 sts, K9.

Row 33: K5, purl across to last 5 sts, K5.

Row 34: K 10, YO, SSK, ★ K 14, YO, SSK; repeat from ★ across to last 10 sts, K 10.

Rows 35-39: Repeat Rows 21 and 22 twice, then repeat Row 21 once **more**.

Row 40: K 18, YO, SSK, ★ K 14, YO, SSK; repeat from ★ across to last 18 sts, K 18.

Repeat Rows 13-40 until Afghan measures approximately 42½" from cast on edge, ending by working Row 24.

Change to small size needles.

Last 6 Rows: Knit across.

Bind off all sts.

Design by Rachael J. Terrill.

17. BABY PULLOVER

Months (size):	3	6	12	18	24
Chest Measurement:	17"	19"	20"	20½"	21"
Finished Chest Measurement:	19"	21"	22"	22½"	23"

Size Note: Instructions are written with sizes 3 months and 6 months in the first set of braces { } and with sizes 12 months, 18 months, and 24 months in the second set of braces. Instructions will be easier to read if you circle all the numbers pertaining to your size. If only one number is given, it applies to all sizes.

MATERIALS

Baby Fingering Weight Yarn: SUPER FINE 1
{2-2½}{2½-3-3½} ounces,
[{60-70}{70-90-100} grams,
{350-440}{440-525-615} yards]
Straight knitting needles, sizes 4 (3.5 mm) **and** 6 (4 mm) **or** sizes needed for gauge
16" Circular needles, size 4 (3.5 mm)
Markers
Cable needle
Buttons - 2
Yarn needle

GAUGE: With large size needles, in Stockinette Stitch, 24 sts and 32 rows = 4"

STITCH GUIDE

CABLE (uses next 9 sts)
Slip next 3 sts onto cable needle and hold in **back** of work, K1 from left needle, K3 from cable needle, K1, slip next st onto cable needle and hold in **front** of work, K3 from left needle, K1 from cable needle.

BACK

RIBBING

With small size needles, cast on {54-60}{62-64-66} sts **loosely**.

Work in K1, P1 ribbing for {1-1}{1½-1½-1½}" increasing 6 sts evenly spaced across last row ***(see Increases, page 43)***: {60-66}{68-70-72} sts.

BODY

Change to large size needles.

Work in Stockinette Stitch until Back measures approximately {9¾-11}{11¾-12½-13½}" from cast on edge, ending by working a **purl** row.

Bind off all sts.

FRONT

RIBBING

With small size needles, cast on {54-60}{62-64-66} sts **loosely**.

Work in K1, P1 ribbing for {1-1}{1½-1½-1½}" increasing 8 sts evenly spaced across last row: {62-68}{70-72-74} sts.

BODY

Change to large size needles.

Row 1 (Right side)**:** K {20-21}{22-23-23}, place marker ***(see Markers, page 43)***, (K1, P1) {11-13}{13-13-14} times, place marker, knit across.

Row 2: Purl across to marker, (K1, P1) across to next marker, purl across.

Row 3: K {11-12}{13-14-14}, work Cable, (P1, K1) across to next marker, work Cable, knit across.

Row 4: Purl across to marker, (P1, K1) across to next marker, purl across.

Row 5: Knit across to marker, (K1, P1) across to next marker, knit across.

Repeat Rows 2-5 for pattern until Front measures approximately {5¼-6}{6¼-7-8}" from cast on edge, ending by working Row 4.

PLACKET OPENING

Note: Maintain established pattern throughout.

Row 1: Knit across to marker, work across {8-10}{10-10-11} sts, bind off next 6 sts, work across: {28-31}{32-33-34} sts **each** side.

Note: Both sides of Placket are worked at the same time, using separate yarn for **each** side.

Row 2: Work across; with second yarn, work across.

Work even until Front measures approximately {7¼-8}{8¾-9½-10½}" from cast on edge, ending by working a **wrong** side row.

NECK SHAPING

Row 1 (Decrease row)**:** Work across to within 2 sts of Neck edge, K2 tog ***(Fig. 6, page 44)***; with second yarn, slip 1 as if to **knit**, K1, PSSO ***(Figs. 8a & b, page 44)***, work across: {27-30}{31-32-33} sts **each** side.

Row 2: Work across; with second yarn, work across.

Repeat Rows 1 and 2, {5-7}{7-7-8} times: {22-23}{24-25-25} sts **each** side.

Work even until Front measures same as Back, ending by working a **wrong** side row.

Bind off remaining sts.

RIGHT PLACKET RIBBING

With **right** side facing and using small size needles, pick up {16-16}{20-20-20} sts evenly spaced along right Placket Opening ***(Fig. 14a, page 46)***.

Work in K1, P1 ribbing for 9 rows.

Bind off all sts in ribbing.

LEFT PLACKET RIBBING

With **right** side facing and using small size needles, pick up {16-16}{20-20-20} sts evenly spaced along left Placket Opening.

Rows 1-4: (K1, P1) across.

Row 5 (Buttonhole row)**:** ★ (K1, P1) {2-2}{3-3-3} times, YO ***(Fig. 13c, page 45)***, P2 tog ***(Fig. 11, page 45)***; repeat from ★ once **more**, (K1, P1) twice.

Rows 6-9: (K1, P1) across.

Bind off all sts in ribbing.

Lapping Left Placket Ribbing over Right Placket Ribbing, sew bottom edges to bound off sts at Placket opening.

SLEEVE (Make 2)

RIBBING

With small size needles, cast on {30-32}{34-36-38} sts **loosely**.

Work in K1, P1 ribbing for {1-1}{1½-1½-1½}" increasing 6 sts evenly spaced across last row: {36-38}{40-42-44} sts.

BODY

Change to large size needles.

Work in Stockinette Stitch increasing one stitch at **each** edge, every {2-2}{2-4-4} rows, {6-2}{2-8-10} times; then increase every {4-4}{4-6-6} rows, {3-7}{8-2-2} times: {54-56}{60-62-68} sts.

Work even until Sleeve measures approximately {5-6}{7-8-9}" from cast on edge, ending by working a **purl** row.

Bind off all sts **loosely**.

FINISHING

Sew shoulder seams.

Sew Sleeves to sweater, matching center of last row on Sleeve to shoulder seam and beginning {4¼-4½}{4¾-5-5½}" down from seam.

Weave underarm and side in one continuous seam ***(Fig. 15, page 46)***.

COLLAR

With **right** side facing and using circular needles, skip Right Placket and pick up {25-29}{29-29-29} sts along right Front Neck edge, pick up {18-22}{22-22-24} sts across Back Neck edge ***(Fig. 14b, page 46)***, pick up {25-29}{29-29-29} sts along left Front Neck edge to Left Placket: {68-80}{80-80-82} sts.

Work in K1, P1 ribbing for 2".

Bind off all sts **loosely** in ribbing.

Sew buttons to Right Placket Ribbing.

Design by Terry Kimbrough.

18. BABY CARDIGAN

Size:	1	2	4
Chest Measurement:	20"	21"	22"
Finished Chest Measurement:	22"	23½"	24"

Size Note: Instructions are written for size 1, with sizes 2 and 4 in braces { }. Instructions will be easier to read if you circle all the numbers pertaining to your size. If only one number is given, it applies to all sizes.

MATERIALS

Sport Weight Yarn:
- White - 3½{4½-5¼} ounces, [100{130-150) grams, 305{395-460) yards]
- Pink - 1½{2-2¼} ounces, [40{60-65} grams, 130{175-195} yards]

Straight knitting needles, sizes 4 (3.5 mm) and 6 (4 mm) **or** sizes needed for gauge
Stitch holders - 3
Yarn needle
Marker
½" Buttons - 5{6-6}

GAUGE: With large size needles, in Stockinette Stitch, 22 sts and 28 rows = 4"

STITCH GUIDE

TWIST

Knit the second stitch on the left needle making sure **not** to drop off left needle ***(Fig. A)***, then knit the first stitch ***(Fig. B)*** slipping both stitches off the left needle.

Fig. A

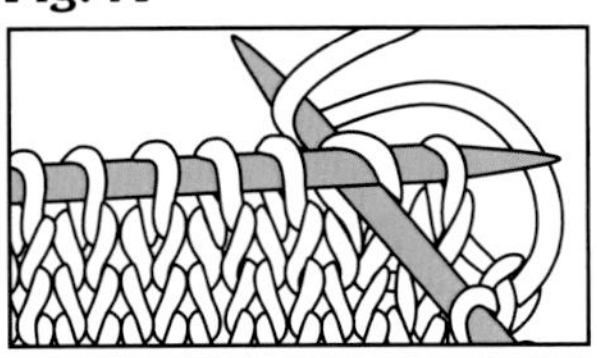

Fig. B

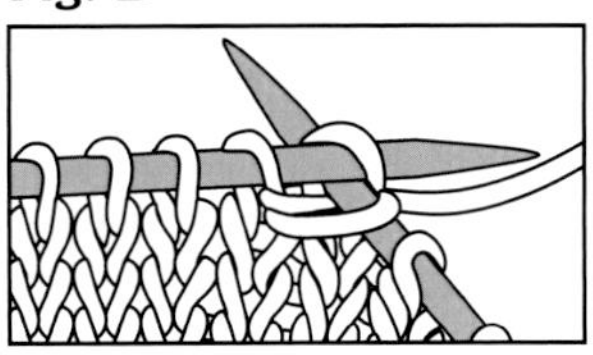

BACK

RIBBING

With small size needles and White, cast on 61{64-67} sts **loosely**.

Row 1: K1, (P2, K1) across.

Row 2: P1, (work Twist, P1) across ***(Figs. A & B)***.

Row 3: K1, (P2, K1) across.

Row 4: P1, (K2, P1) across.

Rows 5-10: Repeat Rows 1-4 once, then repeat Rows 1 and 2 once **more**.

Row 11: Work across in established pattern increasing 2{3-2} sts evenly spaced ***(see Increases, page 43)***: 63{67-69} sts.

BODY

Change to large size needles.

Row 1 (Right side)**:** Knit across.

Row 2: Purl across.

Row 3: K7{3-4}, P1, (K5, P1) across to last 7{3-4) sts, K7{3-4}.

Row 4: Purl across.

Row 5: Knit across.

Row 6: Purl across.

Row 7: K4{6-7}, P1, (K5, P1) across to last 4{6-7} sts, K4{6-7}.

Row 8: Purl across.

Repeat Rows 1-8 until Back measures approximately 7½{8½-9¾}" from cast on edge, ending by working Row 4.

ARMHOLE SHAPING

Row 1: Bind off 3 sts, knit across: 60{64-66} sts.

Row 2: Bind off 3 sts, purl across: 57{61-63} sts.

Row 3: K1, slip 1 as if to **knit**, K1, PSSO (***Figs. 8a & b, page 44***), K4{0-1} ***(see Zeros, page 43)***, P1, (K5, P1) across to last 7{3-4} sts, K4{0-1}, K2 tog ***(Fig. 6, page 44)***, K1: 55{59-61} sts.

Row 4 (Increase row)**:** Purl across increasing 0{2-6} sts evenly spaced; cut White: 55{61-67} sts.

Row 5: With Pink, P1, (K2, P1) across.

Row 6: K1, (P2, K1) across.

Row 7: P1, (work Twist, P1) across.

Row 8: K1, (P2, K1) across.

Row 9: P1, (K2, P1) across.

Repeat Rows 6-9 until Armholes measure approximately 4½{5-5½}", ending by working Row 7.

Next Row: Bind off 12{15-15} sts, (P2, K1) 10{10-12} times, slip 31{31-37} sts just worked onto st holder, bind off remaining sts.

LEFT FRONT

RIBBING

With small size needles and White, cast on 34{37-37} sts **loosely**.

Row 1: K1, (P2, K1) across.

Row 2: (P1, work Twist) across to last st, K1.

Row 3: K1, (P2, K1) across.

Row 4: P1 (K2, P1) across to last 3 sts, K3.

Rows 5-10: Repeat Rows 1-4 once, then repeat Rows 1 and 2 once **more**.

Row 11: K1, (P2, K1) twice (Band), place marker ***(see Markers, page 43)***, work across in established pattern increasing 1{1-2) st(s) evenly spaced: 35{38-39} sts.

BODY

Row 1 (Right side)**:** Knit across to marker, P1, K2, P1, K3.

Row 2: K1, (P2, K1) twice, purl across.

Row 3: K4{7-2}, (P1, K5) across to marker, (P1, work Twist) twice, K1.

Row 4: K1, (P2, K1) twice, purl across.

Row 5: Knit across to marker, P1, K2, P1, K3.

Row 6: K1, (P2, K1) twice, purl across.

Row 7: K7{4-5}, P1, (K5, P1) across to within 2 sts of marker, K2, (P1, work Twist) twice, K1.

Row 8: K1, (P2, K1) twice, purl across.

Repeat Rows 1-8 until Left Front measures same as Back to Armhole Shaping, ending by working Row 4.

ARMHOLE SHAPING

Row 1: Bind off 3 sts, knit across to marker, P1, K2, P1, K3: 32{35-36} sts.

Row 2: K1, (P2, K1) twice, purl across.

Row 3: K1, slip 1 as if to **knit**, K1, PSSO, K1{4-5}, P1, (K5, P1) across to within 2 sts of marker, K2, (P1, work Twist) twice, K1: 31{34-35} sts.

Row 4: K1, (P2, K1) twice (remove marker), purl across increasing 0{0-2} sts evenly spaced; cut White: 31{34-37} sts.

Row 5: With Pink, P1, (K2, P1) across to last 3 sts, K3.

Row 6: K1, (P2, K1) across.

Row 7: (P1, work Twist) across to last st, K1.

Row 8: K1, (P2, K1) across.

Row 9: P1, (K2, P1) across to last 3 sts, K3.

Repeat Rows 6-9 for pattern until Armhole measures approximately 3{3½-4}", ending by working Row 8.

NECK SHAPING

Note: Maintain established pattern throughout.

Row 1: Work across 15{18-18} sts, slip remaining 16{16-19} sts onto st holder.

Row 2: Work across.

Row 3 (Decrease row)**:** Work across to last 2 sts, decrease ***(see Decreases, pages 44 & 45)***: 14{17-17} sts.

Rows 4-7: Repeat Rows 2 and 3 twice: 12{15-15} sts.

Rows 8-12: Work across.

Bind off remaining sts.

Mark Band for 5{6-6} buttons. Place first button on Row 7 of Ribbing. Remembering that the last button will be placed on Row 1 of Neck Ribbing, evenly space remaining 3{4-4} buttons.

RIGHT FRONT

RIBBING

With small size needles and White, cast on 34{37-37} sts **loosely**.

Row 1: K1, (P2, K1) across.

Row 2: K1, (work Twist, P1) across.

Row 3: K1, (P2, K1) across.

Row 4: K3, P1, (K2, P1) across.

Rows 5 and 6: Repeat Rows 1 and 2.

Row 7 (Buttonhole row)**:** (K1, P2) across to last 4 sts, YO ***(Fig. 13c, page 45)***, P2 tog ***(Fig. 11, page 45)***, P1, K1.

Note: Work remaining Buttonholes to match button placement on Left Front.

Row 8: K3, P1, (K2, P1) across.

Row 9: K1, (P2, K1) across.

Row 10: K1, (work Twist, P1) twice (Band), place marker, (work Twist, P1) across.

Row 11: Work across in established pattern to marker increasing 1{1-2} st(s) evenly spaced, K1, (P2, K1) twice: 35{38-39} sts.

BODY

Change to large size needles.

Row 1 (Right side)**:** K3, P1, K2, P1, knit across.

Row 2: Purl across to marker, K1, (P2, K1) twice.

Row 3: K1, (work Twist, P1) twice, (K5, P1) across to last 4{7-2} sts, K4{7-2}.

Row 4: Purl across to marker, K1, (P2, K1) twice.

Row 5: K3, P1, K2, P1, knit across.

Row 6: Purl across to marker, K1, (P2, K1) twice.

Row 7: K1, (work Twist, P1) twice, K2, P1, (K5, P1) across to last 7{4-5} sts, K7{4-5}.

Row 8: Purl across to marker, K1, (P2, K1) twice.

Repeat Rows 1-8 until Right Front measures same as Back to Armhole Shaping, ending by working Row 5.

ARMHOLE SHAPING

Row 1: Bind off 3 sts, purl across to marker, K1, (P2, K1) twice: 32{35-36} sts.

Row 2: K1, (work Twist, P1) twice, K2, P1, (K5, P1) across to last 4{7-8} sts, K1{4-5}, K2 tog, K1: 31{34-35} sts.

Row 3: Purl across to marker increasing 0{0-2} sts evenly spaced (remove marker), K1, (P2, K1) twice; cut White: 31{34-37} sts.

Row 4: With Pink, K3, P1, (K2, P1) across.

Row 5: K1, (P2, K1) across.

Row 6: K1, (work Twist, P1) across.

Row 7: K1, (P2, K1) across.

Row 8: K3, P1, (K2, P1) across.

Repeat Rows 5-8 for pattern until Armhole measures approximately 3{3½-4}", ending by working Row 6.

NECK SHAPING

Note: Maintain established pattern throughout.

Row 1: Work across 15{18-18} sts, slip remaining 16{16-19} sts onto st holder.

Row 2 (Decrease row)**:** Decrease, work across: 14{17-17} sts.

Row 3: Work across.

Rows 4-7: Repeat Rows 2 and 3 twice: 12{15-15} sts.

Rows 8-13: Work across.

Bind off remaining sts.

SLEEVE (Make 2)

RIBBING

With small size needles and White, cast on 34{34-37} sts **loosely**.

Row 1: K1, (P2, K1) across.

Row 2: P1, (work Twist, P1) across.

Row 3: K1, (P2, K1) across.

Row 4: P1, (K2, P1) across.

Rows 5-10: Repeat Rows 1-4 once, then repeat Rows 1 and 2 once **more**.

Row 11: Work across in established pattern increasing 13{17-18} sts evenly spaced: 47{51-55} sts.

BODY

Change to large size needles.

Row 1 (Right side)**:** Knit across.

Row 2: Purl across.

Row 3: K5{7-3}, P1, (K5, P1) across to last 5{7-3} sts, K5{7-3}.

Row 4: Purl across.

Row 5: Knit across.

Row 6: Purl across.

Row 7: K2{4-6}, P1, (K5, P1) across to last 2{4-6} sts, K2{4-6}.

Row 8: Purl across.

Repeat Rows 1-8 until Sleeve measures approximately 7{9¼-10¼}" from cast on edge, ending by working Row 8.

SLEEVE CAP

Row 1: Bind off 3 sts, knit across: 44{48-52} sts.

Row 2: Bind off 3 sts, purl across: 41{45-49} sts.

Row 3: K1, slip 1 as if to **knit**, K1, PSSO, K5{1-3}, P1, (K5, P1) across to last 8{4-6} sts, K5{1-3}, K2 tog, K1: 39{43-47} sts.

Row 4: Purl across increasing 1{3-2} st(s) evenly spaced; cut White: 40{46-49} sts.

Row 5: With Pink, P1, (K2, P1) across.

Row 6: K1, (P2, K1) across.

Row 7: P1, (work Twist, P1) across.

Row 8: K1, (P2, K1) across.

Row 9: P1, (K2, P1) across.

Repeat Rows 6-9 until Sleeve Cap measures approximately 4{4½-5¼}", ending by working Row 8.

SHAPING

Row 1: P1, (K2 tog, P1) across: 27{31-33} sts.

Row 2: P 0{1-0}, P3 tog across ***(Fig. 12, page 45)***: 9{11-11} sts.

Bind off remaining sts **tightly**.

FINISHING

Sew shoulder seams.
Set in Sleeves, matching center of last row on Sleeve to shoulder seam.
Weave underarm and side in one continuous seam ***(Fig. 15, page 46)***.

NECK RIBBING

With **wrong** side facing, slip 16{16-19} sts from Right Front st holder onto small size needle, with Pink, K1, (P2, K1) 5{5-6} times, **turn**; K3, P1, (K2, P1) 4{4-5} times, pick up 11 sts along right Neck edge ***(Fig. 14a, page 46)***, slip 31{31-37} sts from Back st holder onto empty needle, P1, (K2, P1) 10{10-12} times, pick up 11 sts along left Neck edge, slip 16{16-19} sts from Left Front st holder onto empty needle, P1, (K2, P1) 4{4-5} times, K3: 85{85-97} sts.

Row 1 (Buttonhole row)**:** (K1, P2) across to last 4 sts, YO, P2 tog, P1, K1.

Row 2: K1, work Twist, (P1, work Twist) across to last st, K1.

Row 3: K1, (P2, K1) across.

Row 4: K3, P1, (K2, P1) across to last 3 sts, K3.

Row 5: K1, (P2, K1) across.

Row 6: K1, work Twist, (P1, work Twist) across to last st, K1.

Bind off all sts **loosely** in pattern.

Sew buttons to Left Front.

Design by Carole Prior.

19. CHRISTENING SET

Finished Size: Newborn

MATERIALS

Bonnet and Booties

Baby Fingering Yarn:
- **Bonnet** - 1 ounce, (30 grams, 145 yards)
- **Booties** - ½ ounce, (20 grams, 75 yards)

Straight knitting needles, size 2 (2.75 mm) **or** size needed for gauge

Stitch holders - 2 (Booties only)

¼" Ribbon:
- Bonnet - 1¼ yards
- Booties - 1¼ yards

1/8" Ribbon:
- Bonnet - ¾ yard

Yarn needle

Sewing needle and thread

Blanket

Sport Weight Yarn:
- 11 ounces, (310 grams, 1,385 yards)

24" Circular needle, size 8 (5 mm) **or** size needed for gauge

Markers

¼" Ribbon - 5 yards

GAUGE: With Baby Fingering Yarn, in Stockinette Stitch, 28 sts and 40 rows = 4";
With Sport Weight Yarn, in Garter Stitch, 17 sts and 34 rows = 4"

BONNET

BRIM

Cast on 11 sts **loosely**.

Row 1: Slip 1 as if to **purl**, K1, ★ YO ***(Fig. 13b, page 45)***, P2 tog ***(Fig. 11, page 45)***, (K, P, K) **all** in next st; repeat from ★ across: 17 sts.

Row 2 (Right side)**:** (K3, YO, P2 tog) 3 times, K2.

Note: Loop a short piece of yarn around any stitch to mark Row 2 as **right** side.

Row 3: Slip 1 as if to **purl**, K1, (YO, P2 tog, K3) across.

Row 4: K2, ★ slip second st on right needle over first st, K1, slip second st on right needle over first st, YO, P2 tog, K2; repeat from ★ across: 11 sts.

Repeat Rows 1-4 until Brim measures approximately 11" from cast on edge, ending by working Row 4.

Bind off all sts **loosely**.

CROWN

With **right** side facing, pick up 83 sts evenly spaced along straight edge of Brim ***(Fig. 14a, page 46)***.

Rows 1-3: Beginning with a **purl** row, work 3 rows in Stockinette Stitch.

Row 4: K1, (P1, K1) across.

Row 5: P1, (K1, P1) across.

Rows 6-8: Repeat Rows 4 and 5 once, then repeat Row 4 once **more**.

Row 9 (Right side)**:** Knit across.

Note: Right side of Brim is wrong side of Crown.

Row 10 AND ALL WRONG SIDE ROWS: K1, purl across to last st, K1.

Row 11: K1, SSK ***(Figs. 10a-c, page 45)***, ★ † YO ***(Fig. 13a, page 45)***, K2, K2 tog ***(Fig. 6, page 44)***, YO, K1, YO, slip 1 as if to **knit**, K2 tog, PSSO ***(Figs. 9a & b, page 44)***, YO, K1, YO, SSK, K2, YO †, slip 1 as if to **knit**, K2 tog, PSSO; repeat from ★ 3 times **more**, then repeat from † to † once, K2 tog, K1.

Row 13: K1, SSK, ★ † K3, YO, K2 tog, YO, K3, YO, SSK, YO, K3 †, slip 1 as if to **knit**, K2 tog, PSSO; repeat from ★ 3 times **more**, then repeat from † to † once, K2 tog, K1.

Row 15: K1, SSK, ★ † (K2, YO) twice, K2 tog, K1, SSK, (YO, K2) twice †, slip 1 as if to **knit**, K2 tog, PSSO; repeat from ★ 3 times **more**, then repeat from † to † once, K2 tog, K1.

Row 17: K1, SSK, ★ † K1, YO, K3, YO, K2 tog, K1, SSK, YO, K3, YO, K1 †, slip 1 as if to **knit**, K2 tog, PSSO; repeat from ★ 3 times **more**, then repeat from † to † once, K2 tog, K1.

Repeat Rows 10-17 until Crown measures approximately 5" from Brim, ending by working Row 17.

BACK

Row 1: Bind off 27 sts, K5, P 17, K6, purl across to last st, K1: 56 sts.

Row 2: Bind off 27 sts, K5, SSK, YO, K2, K2 tog, YO, K1, YO, slip 1 as if to **knit**, K2 tog, PSSO, YO, K1, YO, SSK, K2, YO, K2 tog, K6: 29 sts.

Row 3 AND ALL WRONG SIDE ROWS: K6, purl across to last 6 sts, K6.

Row 4: K6, SSK, K3, YO, K2 tog, YO, K3, YO, SSK, YO, K3, K2 tog, K6.

Row 6: K6, SSK, (K2, YO) twice, K2 tog, K1, SSK, (YO, K2) twice, K2 tog, K6.

Row 8: K6, SSK, K1, YO, K3, YO, K2 tog, K1, SSK, YO, K3, YO, K1, K2 tog, K6.

Row 10: K6, SSK, YO, K2, K2 tog, YO, K1, YO, slip 1 as if to **knit**, K2 tog, PSSO, YO, K1, YO, SSK, K2, YO, K2 tog, K6.

Repeat Rows 3-10 until Back measures approximately 4".

Bind off all sts **loosely**.

FINISHING

Sew Back seams.

Fold Brim to **right** side.

NECKBAND

With **right** side facing and working through **both** thicknesses at Brim, pick up 62 sts evenly spaced across neck edge.

Rows 1-7: Knit across.

Bind off all sts **loosely**.

Using photo as a guide for placement:
Weave $^{1}/_{8}$" ribbon through inside eyelets of Brim; tack in place.
Weave $^{1}/_{8}$" ribbon through middle eyelets of Brim; tack in place.
Sew on $^{1}/_{4}$" ribbon ties.

BOOTIES

CUFF

Cast on 8 sts **loosely**.

Row 1: Slip 1 as if to **purl**, K1, ★ YO ***(Fig. 13b, page 45)***, P2 tog ***(Fig. 11, page 45)***, (K, P, K) **all** in next st; repeat from ★ once **more**: 12 sts.

Row 2 (Right side)**:** (K3, YO, P2 tog) twice, K2.

Note: Loop a short piece of yarn around any stitch to mark Row 2 as **right** side.

Row 3: Slip 1 as if to **purl**, K1, (YO, P2 tog, K3) twice.

Row 4: K2, ★ slip second st on right needle over first st, K1, slip second st on right needle over first st, YO, P2 tog, K2; repeat from ★ once **more**: 8 sts.

Rows 5-56: Repeat Rows 1-4, 13 times.

Bind off all sts **loosely**.

With **right** side facing pick up 33 sts evenly spaced along straight edge of Cuff (***Fig. 14a, page 46)***.

Beginning with a **purl** row, work 3 rows in Stockinette Stitch.

INSTEP

Row 1: K 11, slip sts just worked onto st holder, K 11, slip remaining sts onto second st holder: 11 sts.

Rows 2-20: Knit across.

Cut yarn.

SIDES

With **right** side facing, slip sts from right st holder onto empty needle, pick up 10 sts along first side of Instep, K 11, pick up 10 sts along second side of Instep, slip 11 sts from left st holder onto empty needle and knit across: 53 sts.

Rows 1-10: Knit across.

Row 11: K3, K2 tog ***(Fig. 6, page 44)***, K 16, K2 tog, K7, K2 tog, K 16, K2 tog K3: 49 sts.

Row 12: Knit across.

Row 13: K3, K2 tog, K 14, K2 tog, K7, K2 tog, K 14, K2 tog, K3: 45 sts.

Row 14: Knit across.

Row 15: K3, K2 tog, K 12, K2 tog, K7, K2 tog, K 12, K2 tog, K3: 41 sts.

Row 16: Knit across.

Bind off all sts **loosely**.

FINISHING

Sew sole and back in one continuous seam.
Using photo as a guide for placement, weave ribbon through bottom eyelets of Cuff and tie in a bow at center front.

BLANKET

Finished Size: 34" x 42½"

CENTER

Cast on 123 sts.

Rows 1-21: Knit across.

Row 22 (Right side)**:** K 11, ★ place marker ***(see Markers, page 43)***, SSK ***(Figs. 10a-c, page 45)***, YO ***(Fig. 13a, page 45)***, K2, K2 tog ***(Fig. 6, page 44)***, YO, K1, YO, slip 1 as if to **knit**, K2 tog, PSSO ***(Figs. 9a & b, page 44)***, YO, K1, YO, SSK, K2, YO, K2 tog, place marker, K 11; repeat from ★ across.

Row 23 AND ALL WRONG SIDE ROWS: (Knit across to next marker, purl across to next marker) 4 times, knit across.

Row 24: ★ Knit across to marker, SSK, K3, YO, K2 tog, YO, K3, YO, SSK, YO, K3, K2 tog; repeat from ★ across to last marker, knit across.

Row 26: ★ Knit across to next marker, SSK, (K2, YO) twice, K2 tog, K1, SSK, (YO, K2) twice, K2 tog; repeat from ★ across to last marker, knit across.

Row 28: ★ Knit across to next marker, SSK, K1, YO, K3, YO, K2 tog, K1, SSK, YO, K3, YO, K1, K2 tog; repeat from ★ across to last marker. knit across.

Repeat Rows 22-29 until Blanket measures approximately 35" from cast on edge, ending by working Row 22.

Next 21 Rows: Knit across.

Bind off all sts.

BORDER

Cast on 11 sts **loosely**.

Row 1: Slip 1 as if **purl**, K1, ★ YO ***(Fig. 13b,page 45)***, P2 tog ***(Fig. 11, page 45)***, (K, P, K) **all** in next st; repeat from ★ across: 17 sts.

Row 2 (Right side)**:** (K3, YO, P2 tog) 3 times, K2.

Note: Loop a short piece of yarn around any stitch to mark Row 2 as **right** side.

Row 3: Slip 1 as if to **purl**, K1, (YO, P2 tog, K3) across.

Row 4: K2, ★ slip second st on right needle over first st, K1, slip second st on right needle over first st, YO, P2 tog, K2; repeat from ★ across: 11 sts.

Repeat Rows 1-4 until Border is long enough to fit completely around center, allowing for ease at corners and ending by working Row 4.

Bind off all sts **loosely**.

FINISHING

Sew straight edge of Border to Center, easing to fit at corners; sew ends together.

Using photo as a guide for placement and beginning at bottom left corner, weave ribbon through inside eyelets of Border and tie in a bow.

Designs by C. Strohmeyer.

---

20. MEN'S SLIPPERS

Size:	**Small**	**Medium**	**Large**
Sole Length:	9½"	10"	10½"

Size Note: Instructions are written for size Small, with sizes Medium and Large in braces { }. Instructions will be easier to read if you circle all the numbers pertaining to your size. If only one number is given, it applies to all sizes.

MATERIALS

Worsted Weight Yarn: (MEDIUM 4)
3½{3¼-4} ounces,
[100{105-110} grams, 200{210-225} yards]
Straight knitting needles, size 9 (5.5 mm)
or size needed for gauge
Crochet hook (for Tie), size I (5.5 mm)
Yarn needle

GAUGE: In Garter Stitch, 4 sts and 8 rows = 1"

HEEL

Cast on 48{50-54} sts **loosely**.

Row 1 (Wrong side)**:** K 16{17-18}, P1 (turning ridge), K 14{14-16}, P1 (turning ridge), knit across.

Row 2 (Eyelet row)**:** K3, K2 tog ***(Fig. 6, page 44)***, YO ***(Fig. 13a, page 45)***, knit across to last 5 sts, YO, K2 tog, K3.

Row 3: K 16{17-18}, P1, K 14{14-16}, P1, knit across.

Row 4: Knit across.

Repeat Rows 1-4 until there are 10{10-11} Eyelet rows, ending by working Row 3.

TOE

Row 1: Bind off 5 sts, knit across: 43{45-49} sts.

Row 2: Bind off 5 sts, K 10{11-12}, P1, K 14{14-16), P1, knit across: 38{40-44) sts.

Row 3: Knit across.

Row 4: K 11{12-13}, P1, K 14{14-16}, P1, knit across.

Repeat Rows 3 and 4 until piece measures approximately 9{9½-10}" from cast on edge.

SHAPING

Row 1 (Decrease row)**:** K2 tog across: 19{20-22} sts.

Row 2: Knit across.

Row 3: K3 tog ***(Fig. 7, page 44)*** 1{0-0} time(s) ***(see Zeros, page 43)***, K2 tog across: 9{10-11} sts.

FINISHING

Cut yarn leaving a long end for sewing. Thread yarn needle with yarn end and separately slip each stitch from the knitting needle onto the yarn; gather the stitches **tightly** and secure end.

Sew center front seam.

Beginning at top edge, sew back seam to turning ridge; weave yarn through remaining sts; gather the stitches **tightly** and secure end.

TIE

Using crochet hook, chain desired length ***(see Crochet Stitches, page 47)***; finish off.

Weave Tie through Eyelet row and tie in front.

Design by Bev Dillon.

21. WOMEN'S SLIPPERS

Size:	Small	Medium	Large
Sole Length:	9"	9½"	10"

Size Note: Instructions are written for size Small with sizes Medium and Large in braces { }. Instructions will be easier to read if you circle all the numbers pertaining to your size. If only one number is given, it applies to all sizes.

MATERIALS

Worsted Weight Yarn: (MEDIUM 4)
3¼{3½-3¾} ounces,
[95{100-105} grams, 185{200-210} yards]
Straight knitting needles, size 9 (5.5 mm)
or size needed for gauge
Yarn needle

GAUGE: In Garter Stitch, 4 sts and 8 rows = 1"

SLIPPER

Beginning at Heel, cast on 32{36-38} sts **loosely**.

Work in Garter Stitch until piece measures approximately 6¾{7¼-7¾}".

SHAPING

Row 1 (Decrease row)**:** K2 tog ***(Fig. 6, page 44)***, knit across to last 2 sts, K2 tog: 30{34-36} sts.

Row 2: Knit across.

Rows 3-10: Repeat Rows 1 and 2, 4 times: 22{26-28} sts.

Cut yarn leaving a long end for sewing. Thread yarn needle with yarn end and separately slip each stitch from the knitting needle onto the yarn; gather the stitches **tightly** and secure end. Sew center front seam to within 4{4¼-4½}" of cast on edge or to desired opening.

RUFFLE CUFF

With **right** side facing, pick up one stitch in end of each row along opening ***(Fig. 14a, page 46)***.

Row 1 (Increase row)**:** Knit into **front** and **back** of each st across ***(Figs. 3a & b, page 43)***.

Rows 2-6: Knit across.

Bind off all sts **loosely**.

Sew back seam.

Design by Ruth Shepherd.

22. DIAMONDS AFGHAN & PILLOW

Finished Size: Afghan - 44" x 59"
Pillow - 14" square

MATERIAIS

Afghan
Worsted Weight Yarn: (MEDIUM 4)
54 ounces, (1,530 grams, 3,050 yards)
29" Circular needle, size 17 (12.75 mm)
or size needed for gauge
Cable needle
Crochet hook for fringe

Pillow
Worsted Weight Yarn: (MEDIUM 4)
9 ounces, (260 grams, 510 yards)
Straight knitting needles, size 8 (5 mm)
or size needed for gauge
Cable needle
14" Pillow form
Fabric - ½ yard for lining
Sewing needle and thread
Yarn needle

Note: Entire Afghan is worked holding two strands of yarn together and Pillow is worked with one strand.

GAUGE: In Stockinette Stitch,
for Afghan, 9 sts and 12 rows= 4";
for Pillow, 18 sts and 24 rows= 4"

STITCH GUIDE

TWIST (uses next 2 sts)
Knit the second stitch on the left needle making sure not to drop off left needle, then knit the first stitch, slipping both stitches off the left needle ***(Figs. A & B, page 32)***.

BACK CABLE (uses next 6 sts)
Slip next 3 sts onto cable needle and hold in **back** of work, K3 from left needle, K3 from cable needle.

FRONT CABLE (uses next 6 sts)
Slip next 3 sts onto cable needle and hold in **front** of work, K3 from left needle, K3 from cable needle.

AFGHAN

Cast on 121 sts **loosely**.

Row 1 AND ALL WRONG SIDE ROWS: K1, P2, K2, P9, K2, P2, ★ K2, P 13, K2, P2, K2, P9, K2, P2; repeat from ★ across to last st, K1.

Row 2: K1, work Twist, P2, K9, P2, work Twist, ★ P2, K5, K2 tog ***(Fig. 6, page 44)***, YO ***(Fig. 13a, page 45)***, K6, P2, work Twist, P2, K9, P2, work Twist; repeat from ★ across to last st, K1.

Note: When instructed to slip a stitch, always slip as if to **knit**.

Row 4: K1, work Twist, P2, work Back Cable, K3, P2, work Twist, ★ P2, K4, K2 tog, YO, K1, YO, slip 1, K1, PSSO ***(Figs. 8a & b, page 44)***, K4, P2, work Twist, P2, work Back Cable, K3, P2, work Twist; repeat from ★ across to last st, K1.

Row 6: K1, work Twist, P2, K9, P2, work Twist, ★ P2, K3, K2 tog, YO, K3, YO, slip 1, K1, PSSO, K3, P2, work Twist, P2, K9, P2, work Twist; repeat from ★ across to last st, K1.

Row 8: K1, work Twist, P2, K3, work Front Cable, P2, work Twist, ★ P2, K2, K2 tog, YO, K5, YO, slip 1, K1, PSSO, K2, P2, work Twist, P2, K3, work Front Cable, P2, work Twist; repeat from ★ across to last st, K1.

Row 10: K1, work Twist, P2, K9, P2, work Twist, ★ P2, K1, K2 tog, YO, K7, YO, slip 1, K1, PSSO, K1, P2, work Twist, P2, K9, P2, work Twist; repeat from ★ across to last st, K1.

Row 12: K1, work Twist, P2, work Back Cable, K3, P2, work Twist,★ P2, K3, YO, slip 1, K1, PSSO, K3, K2 tog, YO, K3, P2, work Twist, P2, work Back Cable, K3, P2, work Twist; repeat from ★ across to last st, K1.

Row 14: K1, work Twist, P2, K9, P2, work Twist, ★ P2, K4, YO, slip 1, K1, PSSO, K1, K2 tog, YO, K4, P2, work Twist, P2, K9, P2, work Twist; repeat from ★ across to last st, K1.

Row 16: K1, work Twist, P2, K3, work Front Cable, P2, work Twist, ★ P2, K5, YO, slip 1, K2 tog, PSSO ***(Figs. 9a & b, page 44)***, YO, K5, P2, work Twist, P2, K3, work Front Cable, P2, work Twist; repeat from ★ across to last st, K1.

Repeat Rows 1-16 until Afghan measures approximately 59" from cast on edge, ending by working Row 16.

Bind off all sts **loosely**.

Holding 8 strands of yarn together, add fringe evenly across short edges of Afghan (***Figs. 17a & b, page 47)***.

PILLOW

FRONT

Cast on 65 sts **loosely**.

Row 1 AND ALL WRONG SIDE ROWS: K4, P2, K3, P9, K3, P2, K3, P 13, K3, P2, K3, P9, K3, P2, K4.

Row 2: K1, P3, work Twist, P3, K9, P3, work Twist, P3, K5, K2 tog ***(Fig. 6, page 44)***, YO ***(Fig. 13a, page 45)***, K6, P3, work Twist, P3, K9, P3, work Twist, P3, K1.

Note: When instructed to slip a stitch, always slip as if to **knit**.

Row 4: K1, P3, work Twist, P3, work Back Cable, K3, P3, work Twist, P3, K4, K2 tog, YO, K1, YO, slip 1, K1, PSSO ***(Figs. 8a & b, page 44)***, K4, P3, work Twist, P3, work Back Cable, K3, P3, work Twist, P3, K1.

Row 6: K1, P3, work Twist, P3, K9, P3, work Twist, P3, K3, K2 tog, YO, K3, YO, slip 1, K1, PSSO, K3, P3, work Twist, P3, K9, P3, work Twist, P3, K1.

Row 8: K1, P3, work Twist, P3, K3, work Front Cable, P3, work Twist, P3, K2, K2 tog, YO, K5, YO, slip 1, K1, PSSO, K2, P3, work Twist, P3, K3, work Front Cable, P3, work Twist, P3, K1.

Row 10: K1, P3, work Twist, P3, K9, P3, work Twist, P3, K1, K2 tog, YO, K7, YO, slip 1, K1, PSSO, K1, P3, work Twist, P3, K9, P3, work Twist, P3, K1.

Row 12: K1, P3, work Twist, P3, work Back Cable, K3, P3, work Twist, P3, K3, YO, slip 1, K1, PSSO, K3, K2 tog, YO, K3, P3, work Twist, P3, work Back Cable, K3, P3, work Twist, P3, K1.

Row 14: K1, P3, work Twist, P3, K9, P3, work Twist, P3, K4, YO, slip 1, K1, PSSO, K1, K2 tog, YO, K4, P3, work Twist, P3, K9, P3, work Twist, P3, K1.

Row 16: K1, P3, work Twist, P3, K3, work Front Cable, P3, work Twist, P3, K5, YO, slip 1, K2 tog, PSSO ***(Figs. 9a & b, page 44)***, YO, K5, P3, work Twist, P3, K3, work Front Cable, P3, work Twist, P3, K1.

Rows 17-97: Repeat Rows 1-16, 5 times; then repeat Row 1 once **more**.

Bind off all sts **loosely**.

BACK

Cast on 63 sts **loosely**.

Beginning with a **purl** row, work in Stockinette Stitch until Back measures same as Front, ending by working a **purl** row.

Bind off all sts **loosely**.

FINISHING

Cut two 15½" squares of fabric.

With **right** sides together and allowing ¼" seam allowance, sew seam leaving an opening at one side. Clip corners, then turn right side out.
Insert pillow form and sew opening closed.

ASSEMBLY

With **wrong** sides of Front and Back together, sew seam inserting pillow form before closing.

Designs by Mary Jane Protus.

23. CABLES AFGHAN

Finished Size: 49" x 65"

MATERIALS

Worsted Weight Yarn: (MEDIUM 4)
58½ ounces, (1,660 grams, 3,845 yards)
29" Circular needles, size 17 (12. 75 mm)
or size needed for gauge
Cable needle
Crochet hook for fringe

Note: Entire Afghan is worked holding two strands of yarn together.

GAUGE: In Stockinette Stitch, 9 sts and 12 rows= 4"

STITCH GUIDE

BACK CABLE (uses next 4 sts)
Slip next 2 sts onto cable needle and hold in **back** of work, K2 from left needle, K2 from cable needle.

FRONT CABLE (uses next 4 sts)
Slip next 2 sts onto cable needle and hold in **front** of work, K2 from left needle, K2 from cable needle.

CLUSTER
K3 tog ***(Fig. 7, page 44)*** but do **not** slip sts off the left needle, YO ***(Fig. 13a page 45)***, knit same 3 sts together again, slipping all 3 sts off the left needle.

AFGHAN

Cast on 162 sts **loosely**.

Row 1: K2, P8, ★ K1, (P3, K1) 4 times, P8; repeat from ★ across to last 2 sts, K2.

Row 2 (Right side)**:** K4, work Back Cable, ★ K2, P1, (K3, P1) 4 times, K2, work Back Cable; repeat from ★ across to last 4 sts, K4.

Row 3: K2, P8, ★ K1, (P3, K1) 4 times, P8; repeat from ★ across to last 2 sts, K2.

Row 4: K2, work Back Cable, work Front Cable, ★ P1, (work Cluster, P1) 4 times, work Back Cable, work Front Cable; repeat from ★ across to last 2 sts, K2.

Row 5: K2, P8, ★ K1, (P3, K1) 4 times, P8; repeat from ★ across to last 2 sts, K2.

Row 6: K 10, P1, K1, P1, (K3, P1) 3 times, K1, P1, ★ K8, P1, K1, P1, (K3, P1) 3 times, K1, P1; repeat from ★ across to last 10 sts, K 10.

Row 7: K2, P8, ★ K1, P1, K1, (P3, K1) 3 times, P1, K1, P8; repeat from ★ across to last 2 sts, K2.

Row 8: K2, work Front Cable, work Back Cable, ★ P1, K1, P1, (work Cluster, P1) 3 times, K1, P1, work Front Cable, work Back Cable; repeat from ★ across to last 2 sts, K2.

Row 9: K2, P8, ★ K1, P1, K1, (P3, K1) 3 times, P1, K1, P8; repeat from ★ across to last 2 sts, K2.

Repeat Rows 2-9 until Afghan measures approximately 65" from cast on edge, ending by working Row 2.

Bind off all sts.

Holding 8 strands of yarn together, add fringe evenly across short edges of Afghan ***(Figs. 17a & b, page 47)***.

Design by Mary Jane Protus.

24. MEN'S PULLOVER

Size:	**36**	**38**	**40**	**42**
Chest Measurement:	36"	38"	40"	44"
Finished Chest Measurement:	40"	42"	44"	46"

Size Note: Instructions are written with sizes 36 and 38 in the first set of braces { } and with sizes 40, 42, and 44 in the second set of braces. Instructions will be easier to read if you circle all the numbers pertaining to your size. If only one number in given, it applies to all sizes.

MATERIALS

Worsted Weight Yarn: (MEDIUM 4)
{23-25}{26-28-30} ounces,
[{650-710}{740-800-850} grams,
{1,335-1,450}{1,510-1,625-1,740} yards]
Straight knitting needles, sizes 5 (3.75 mm) **and** 7 (4.5 mm) **or** sizes needed for gauge
16" Circular needle, size 5 (3. 75 mm)
Stitch holders - 2
Markers
Yarn needle

GAUGE: With large size needles, in Stockinette Stitch, 20 sts and 26 rows = 4"

BACK

RIBBING

With small size needles, cast on {102-108}{112-118-124} sts **loosely**.

Work in K1, P1 ribbing for 2".

BODY

Change to large size needles.

Work in Stockinette Stitch until Back measures approximately {24½-26}{26½-27-27½}" from cast on edge, ending by working a **knit** row.

SHOULDER SHAPING

Rows 1 and 2: Bind off {11-12}{13-14-14} sts at the beginning of the next 2 rows, work across: {80-84}{86-90-96} sts.

Rows 3 and 4: Bind off {12-12}{13-14-15} sts at the beginning of the next 2 rows, work across: {56-60}{60-62-66} sts.

Rows 5 and 6: Bind off {12-13}{13-14-15) sts at the beginning of the next 2 rows, work across: {32-34}{34-34-36} sts.

Slip remaining sts onto st holder; cut yarn.

FRONT

Work same as Back until Front measures approximately {21½-23}{23½-23½-24}" from cast on edge, ending by working a **knit** row.

NECK SHAPING

Note: Both sides of Neck are worked at the same time, using separate yarn for **each** side.

Row 1: Purl {41-43}{45-48-50} sts, slip next {20-22}{22-22-24} sts onto st holder; with second yarn, purl across: {41-43}{45-48-50} sts **each** side.

Row 2 (Decrease row)**:** Knit across to within 2 sts of Neck edge, K2 tog ***(Fig. 6, page 44)***; with second yarn, slip 1 as if to **knit**, K1, PSSO ***(Figs. 8a & b, page 44)***, knit across: {40-42}{44-47-49} sts **each** side.

Row 3 (Decrease row)**:** Purl across to within 2 sts of Neck edge, P2 tog ***(Fig. 11, page 45)***; with second yarn, P2 tog, purl across: {39-41}{43-46-48} sts **each** side.

Row 4 (Decrease row)**:** Knit across to within 2 sts of Neck edge, K2 tog; with second yarn, slip 1 as if to **knit**, K1, PSSO, knit across: {38-40}{42-45-47} sts **each** side.

Row 5: Purl across; with second yarn, purl across.

Rows 6-11: Repeat Rows 4 and 5, 3 times: {35-37}{39-42-44} sts **each** side.

Work even until Front measures same as Back to Shoulder Shaping, ending by working a **purl** row.

SHOULDER SHAPING

Rows 1 and 2: Bind off {11-12}{13-14-14} sts at Armhole edge, work across; with second yarn, work across: {24-25}{26-28-30} sts **each** side.

Rows 3 and 4: Bind off {12-12}{13-14-15} sts at Armhole edge, work across; with second yarn, work across: {12-13}{13-14-15} sts **each** side.

Row 5: Bind off {12-13}{13-14-15} sts; with second yarn, work across.

Bind off remaining sts.

SLEEVE (Make 2)

RIBBING

With small size needles, cast on {44-44}{44-46-48} sts **loosely**.

Work in K1, P1 ribbing for 2½", increasing 8 sts evenly spaced across last row ***(see Increases, page 43)***: {52-52}{52-54-56} sts.

BODY

Change to large size needles.

Row 1 (Right side)**:** Knit across.

Row 2: Purl across.

Row 3 (Increase row)**:** K1, increase, knit across to last 2 sts, increase, K1: {54-54}{54-56-58} sts.

Working in Stockinette Stitch, continue to increase one stitch at **each** edge in same manner, every other row, {0-2}{5-9-10} times **more *(see Zeros, page 43)***; then increase every fourth row, {19-20}{19-17-17} times: {92-98}{102-108-112} sts.

Work even until Sleeve measures approximately {17¼-17½}{17¾-18-18¼}" from cast on edge or desired length to underarm, ending by working a **purl** row.

SLEEVE CAP

Bind off 5 sts at the beginning of the next {16-18}{18-20-20) rows, work across: {12-8}{12-8-12} sts.

Bind off remaining sts.

FINISHING

Sew shoulder seams.

NECK RIBBING

With **right** side facing and using circular needles, knit {32-34}{34-34-36} sts from Back st holder, pick up {24-24}{24-25-26} sts along left Front Neck edge ***(Fig. 14a, page 46)***, knit {20-22}{22-22-24} sts from Front st holder, pick up {24-24}{24-25-26} sts along right Front Neck edge, place marker for beginning of rnd ***(see Markers, page 43)***: {100-104}{104-106-112} sts.

Work in K1, P1 ribbing around for 1".

Bind off all sts **loosely** in ribbing.

Sew Sleeves to sweater, matching center of last row on Sleeve to shoulder seam and beginning {9½-10}{10½-11-11½}" down from seam.

Weave underarm and side in one continuous seam ***(Fig. 15, page 46)***.

GENERAL INSTRUCTIONS

ABBREVIATIONS

ch(s)	chain(s)
FC	Front Cross
K	knit
mm	millimeters
p	purl
PSSO	pass slipped stitch over
Rnd(s)	Round(s)
SC	single crochet(s)
SSK	slip, slip, knit
st(s)	stitch(es)
tog	together
YO	yarn over

SYMBOLS & TERMS

★ — work instructions following ★ as many **more** times as indicated in addition to the first time.

† to † — work all instructions from first † to second † **as many** times as specified.

( ) or [ ] — work enclosed instructions **as many** times as specified by the number immediately following **or** work all enclosed instructions in the stitch indicated **or** contains explanatory remarks.

colon(:) — the number(s) given after a colon at the end of a row or round denote(s) the number of stitches you should have on that row or round.

work even — work without increasing or decreasing in the established pattern.

GAUGE

Exact gauge is **essential** for proper size or fit. Before beginning your project, make a sample swatch in the stitch, yarn, and needles specified. After completing the swatch, measure it, counting your stitches and rows carefully. If your swatch is larger or smaller than specified, **make another, changing needle size to get the correct gauge**. Keep trying until you find the size needles that will give you the specified gauge. Once proper gauge is obtained, measure width of piece approximately every 3" to be sure gauge remains consistent.

YARN

The projects shown can be made with any yarn in the weight specified, as long as the correct gauge can be obtained.

A baby fingering weight yarn is any yarn that lists gauge on the label as 7 sts = 1" in Stockinette Stitch.
A sport weight yarn is any yarn that lists gauge on the label as 6 sts = 1" in Stockinette Stitch.
A worsted weight yarn is any yarn that lists gauge on the label as 5 sts = 1" in Stockinette Stitch.
A bulky weight yarn is any yarn that lists gauge on the label as 3 sts = 1" in Stockinette Stitch.

It is best to refer to the **yardage** to determine how many balls or skeins to purchase. Remember, in order for your project to be the correct size, it is not the brand of yarn that matters, but the GAUGE that is important.

KNIT TERMINOLOGY		
UNITED STATES		INTERNATIONAL
gauge	=	tension
bind off	=	cast off
yarn over (YO)	=	yarn forward (yfwd) **or** yarn around needle (yrn)

Yarn Weight Symbol & Names	LACE 0	SUPER FINE 1	FINE 2	LIGHT 3	MEDIUM 4	BULKY 5	SUPER BULKY 6	JUMBO 7
Type of Yarns in Category	Fingering, size 10 crochet thread	Sock, Fingering, Baby	Sport, Baby	DK, Light Worsted	Worsted, Afghan, Aran	Chunky, Craft, Rug	Super Bulky, Roving	Jumbo, Roving
Knit Gauge Ranges in Stockinette St to 4" (10 cm)	33-40 sts**	27-32 sts	23-26 sts	21-24 sts	16-20 sts	12-15 sts	7-11 sts	6 sts and fewer
Advised Needle Size Range	000 to 1	1 to 3	3 to 5	5 to 7	7 to 9	9 to11	11 to 17	17 and larger

* GUIDELINES ONLY: The chart above reflects the most commonly used gauges and needle sizes for specific yarn categories.

** Lace weight yarns are usually knitted on larger needles to create lacy openwork patterns. Accordingly, a gauge range is difficult to determine. Always follow the gauge stated in your pattern.

KNITTING NEEDLES																			
U.S.	0	1	2	3	4	5	6	7	8	9	10	10½	11	13	15	17	19	35	50
U.K.	13	12	11	10	9	8	7	6	5	4	3	2	1	00	000	---	---	---	---
Metric - mm	2	2.25	2.75	3.25	3.5	3.75	4	4.5	5	5.5	6	6.5	8	9	10	12.75	15	19	25

SIZING

When choosing what size to make, you may want to measure a favorite garment with similar styling and knit the size that has the nearest finished measurement.

Once you have chosen a size, you may need to adjust the body length and sleeve length to accommodate actual measurement.

MARKERS

As a convenience to you, we have used markers to help distinguish the beginning of a pattern or the beginning of a round. Place markers as instructed. You may use purchased markers or tie a length of contrasting color yarn around the needle. When you reach a marker on each row or round, slip it from the left needle to the right needle; remove it when no longer needed.

ZEROS

To consolidate the length of an involved pattern, zeros are sometimes used so that all sizes can be combined. For example, K4{0-1} means size Small would K4, size Medium would do nothing, and size Large would K1.

BASIC STITCHES

STOCKINETTE STITCH

Knit one row (right side), purl one row. The knit side is smooth and flat ***(Fig. la)***, and the purl side is bumpy ***(Fig. lb)***.

Fig. la

Fig. lb

GARTER STITCH

Knit every row. Two rows of knitting make one horizontal ridge in your fabric ***(Fig. 2)***.

Fig. 2

SEED STITCH

Knit the purl stitches and purl the knit stitches as they face you.

INCREASES

INCREASING EVENLY ACROSS A ROW

This method eliminates the increase stitch at the beginning and the end of the row, creating a smooth line for sewing the seam. Add one to the number of increases required and divide that number into the number of stitches on the needle. Subtract one from the result and the new number is the approximate number of stitches to be worked **between** each increase. Adjust the number as needed.

KNIT INCREASE

Knit the next stitch but do **not** slip it off the left needle ***(Fig. 3a)***. Instead, knit into the **back** of the **same** stitch ***(Fig. 3b)***, then slip it off the left needle.

Fig. 3a

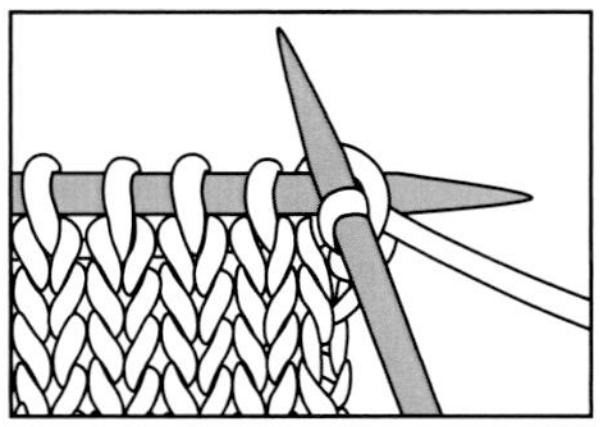

Fig. 3b

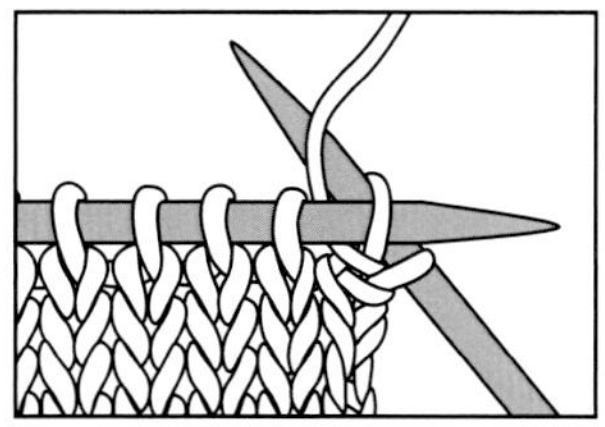

PURL INCREASE

Purl the next stitch but do **not** slip it off the left needle. Insert the right needle into the **back** loop of the **same** stitch from back to front ***(Fig. 4)*** and purl it. Slip it off the needle.

Fig. 4

ADDING NEW STITCHES

If you are adding new stitches in the middle or at the end of a row, turn work around so needles are reversed. Insert right needle into stitch as if to **knit**, yarn over and pull loop through ***(Fig. 5a)***, insert left needle into loop just worked from **front** to **back** and slip onto left needle ***(Fig. 5b)***. Repeat for required number of stitches.

Fig. 5a

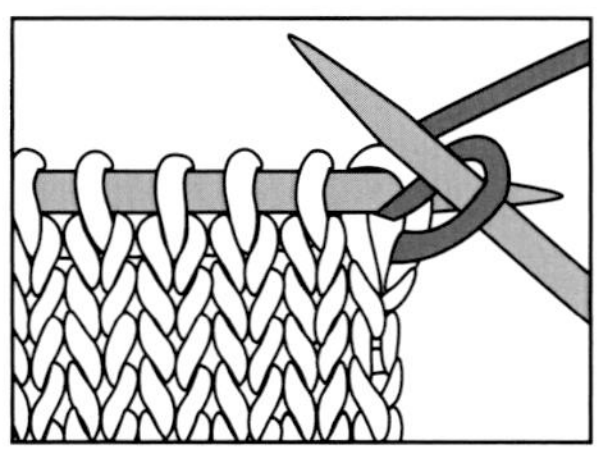

Fig. 5b

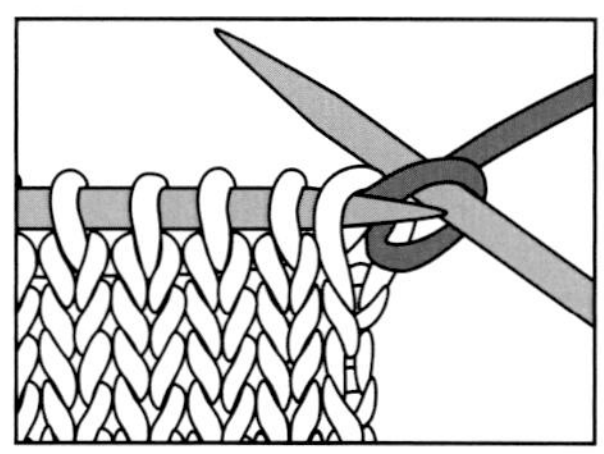

DECREASES

DECREASING EVENLY ACROSS A ROW

This method eliminates the decrease stitch at the beginning and the end of the row, creating a smooth line for sewing the seam. Add one to the number of decreases required and divide that number into the number of stitches on the needle. Subtract 2 from the result and the new number is the approximate number of stitches to be worked **between** each decrease. Adjust the number as needed.

KNIT 2 TOGETHER *(abbreviated K2 tog)*

Insert the right needle into the **front** of the first two stitches on the left needle as if to **knit** ***(Fig. 6)***, then **knit** them together.

Fig. 6

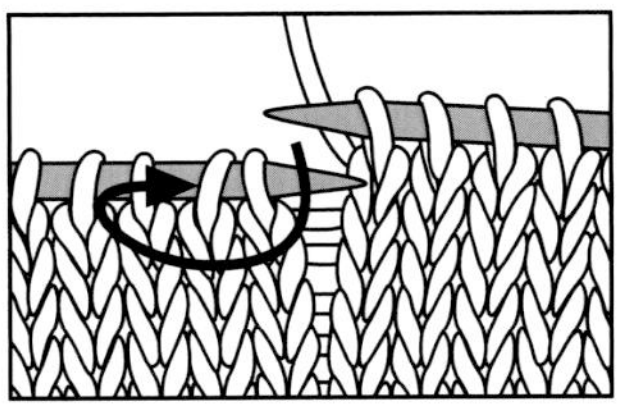

KNIT 3 TOGETHER *(abbreviated K3 tog)*

Insert the right needle into the **front** of the first three stitches on the left needle as if to **knit** ***(Fig. 7)***, then **knit** them together.

Fig.7

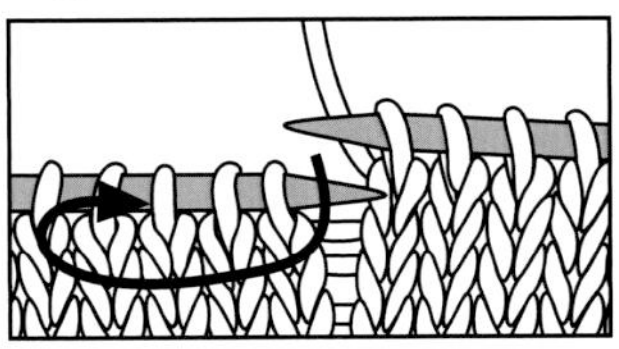

SLIP 1, KNIT 1, PASS SLIPPED STITCH OVER

(abbreviated slip 1, K1, PSSO)

Slip one stitch as if to **knit** ***(Fig. 8a)***, then knit the next stitch. With the left needle, bring the slipped stitch over the knit stitch ***(Fig. 8b)*** and off the needle.

Fig. 8a

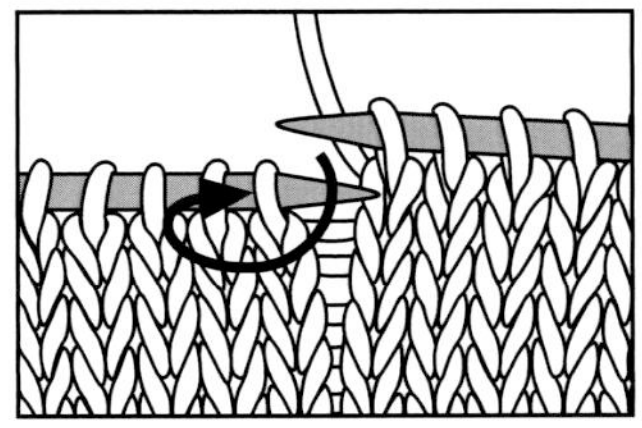

Fig. 8b

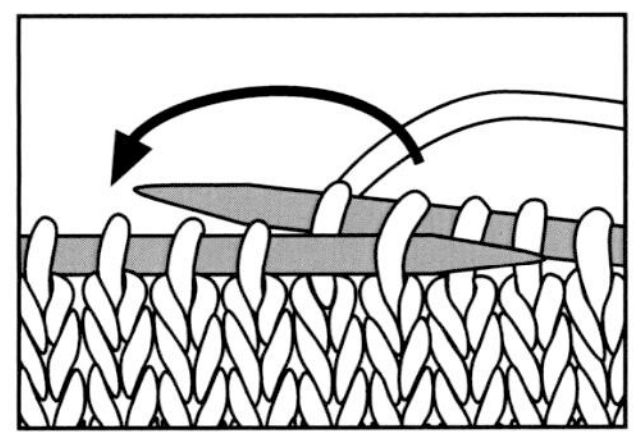

SLIP 1, KNIT 2 TOGETHER, PASS SLIPPED STITCH OVER

(abbreviated slip 1, K2 tog, PSSO)

Slip one stitch as if to **knit** ***(Fig. 9a)***, then knit the next two stitches together. With the left needle, bring the slipped stitch over the stitch just made ***(Fig. 9b)*** and off the needle.

Fig. 9a

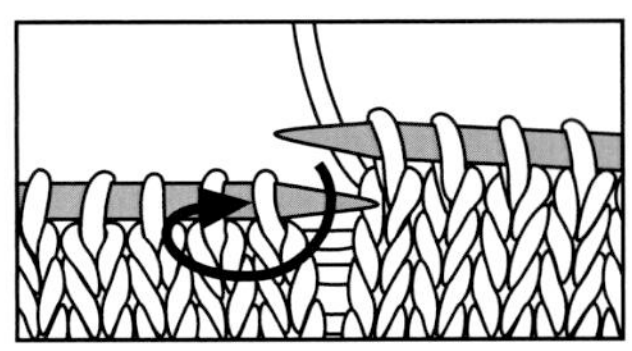

Fig. 9b

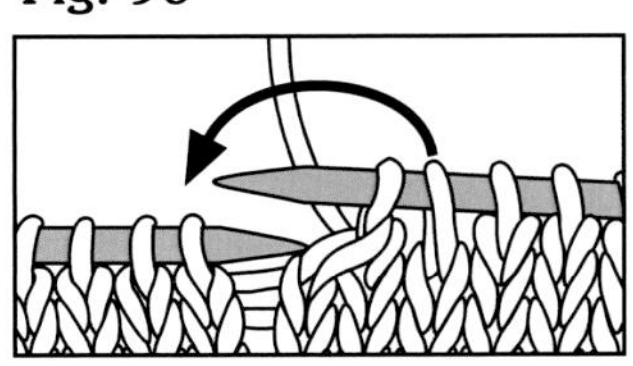

SLIP, SLIP, KNIT *(abbreviated SSK)*

With yarn in back of work, separately slip two stitches as if to **knit** ***(Fig. 10a)***. Insert the **left** needle into the **front** of both slipped sts ***(Fig. 10b)*** and knit them together ***(Fig. 10c)***.

Fig. 10a

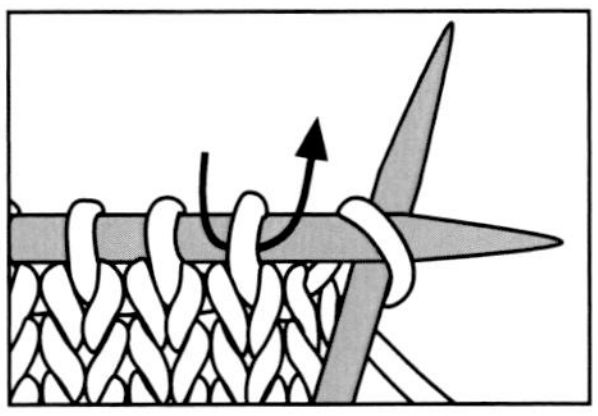

Fig. 10b

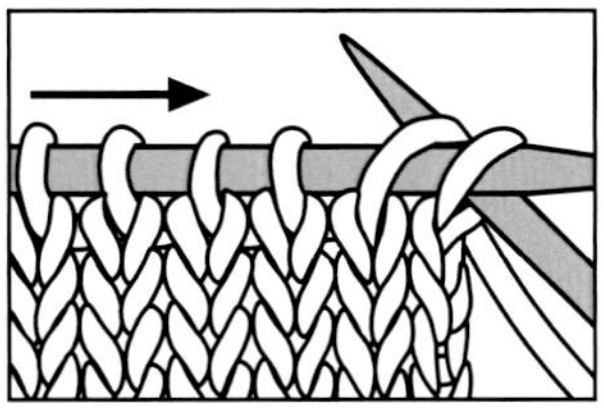

Fig. 10c

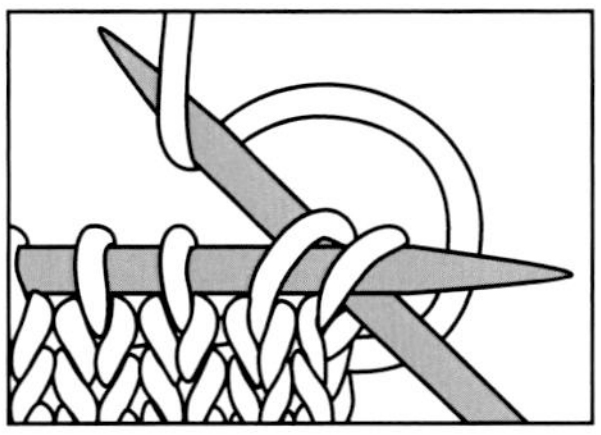

PURL 2 TOGETHER *(abbreviated P2 tog)*

Insert the right needle into the front of the first two stitches on the left needle as if to purl ***(Fig. 11)***, then purl them together.

Fig. 11

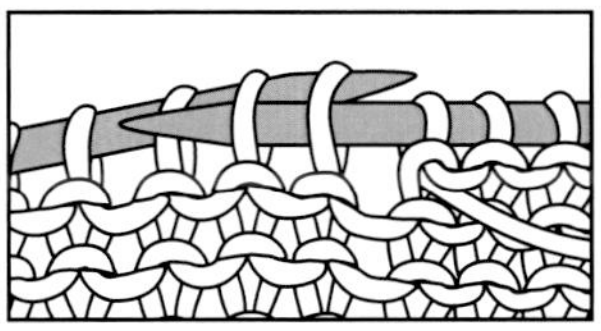

PURL 3 TOGETHER *(abbreviated P3 tog)*

Insert the right needle into the **front** of the first three sts on the left needle as if to **purl** ***(Fig. 12)***, then **purl** them together.

Fig. 12

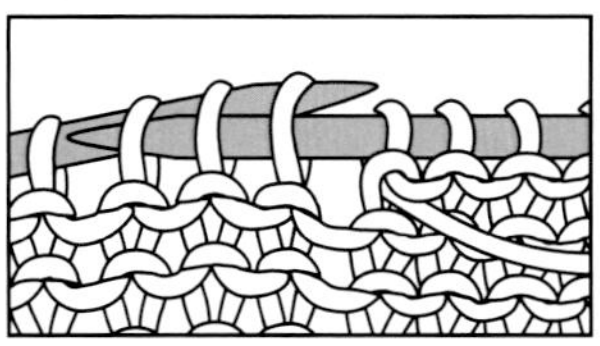

YARN OVERS

After a knit stitch, before a knit stitch

Bring the yarn forward **between** the needles, then back **over** the top of the right hand needle, so that it is now in position to knit the next stitch ***(Fig. 13a)***.

Fig. 13a

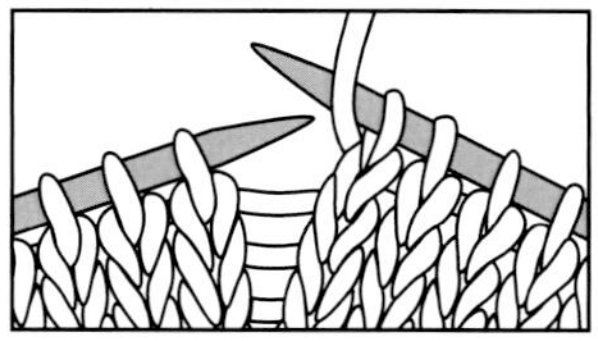

After a knit stitch, before a purl stitch

Bring the yarn forward **between** the needles, then back **over** the top of the right hand needle and forward **between** the needles again, so that it is now in position to purl the next stitch ***(Fig. 13b)***.

Fig. 13b

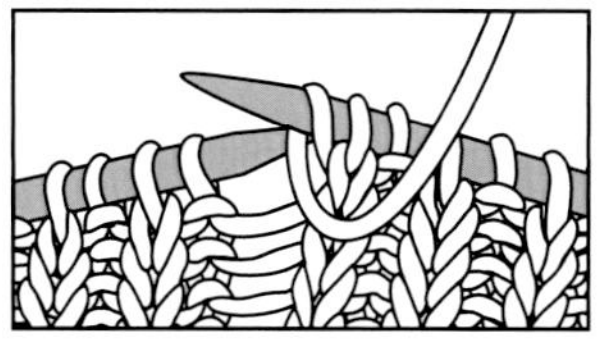

After a purl stitch, before a purl stitch

Take yarn over the right hand needle to the back, then forward **under** it, so that it is now in posititon to purl the next stitch ***(Fig. 13c)***.

Fig. 13c

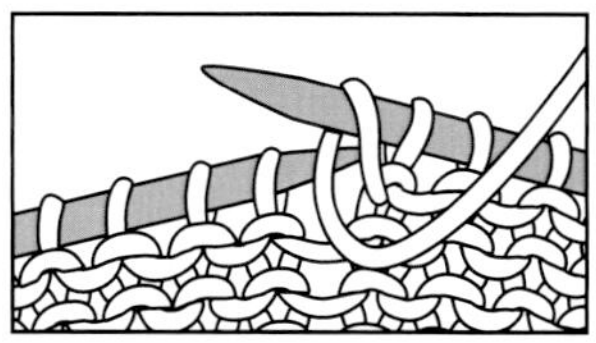

PICKING UP STITCHES

When instructed to pick up stitches, insert the needle from the **front** to the **back** under two strands at the edge of the worked piece ***(Figs. 14a & b)***. Put the yarn around the needle as if to **knit**, then bring the needle with the yarn back through the stitch to the right side, resulting in a stitch on the needle. Repeat this along the edge, picking up the required number of stitches.
A crochet hook may be helpful to pull yarn through.

Fig. 14a

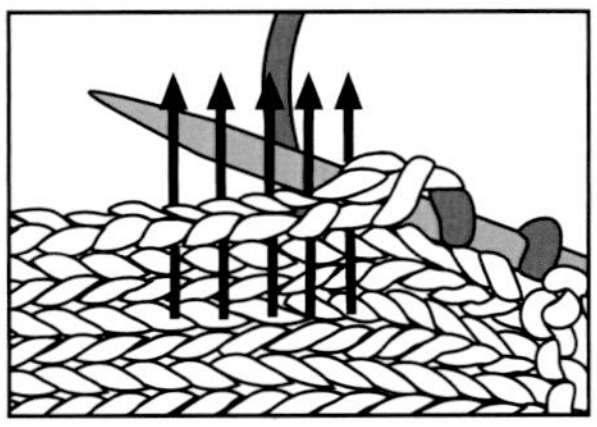

Fig. 14b

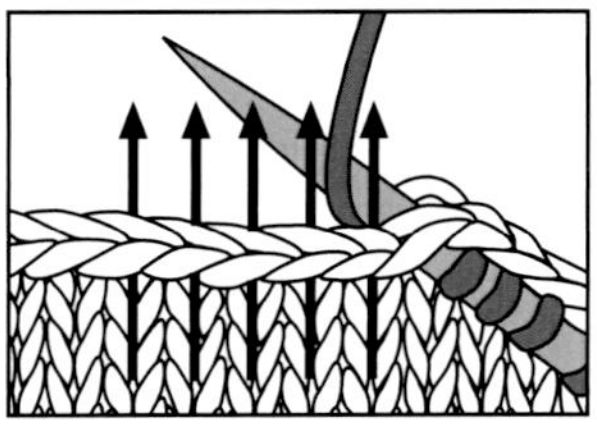

WEAVING SEAMS

With the **right** side of both pieces facing you and the edges even, sew through both sides once to secure the seam. Insert the needle under the bar **between** the first and second stitches on the row and pull the yarn through ***(Fig. 15)***. Insert the needle under the next bar on the second side. Repeat from side to side, being careful to match rows. If the edges are different lengths, it may be necessary to insert the needle under two bars at one edge.

Fig. 15

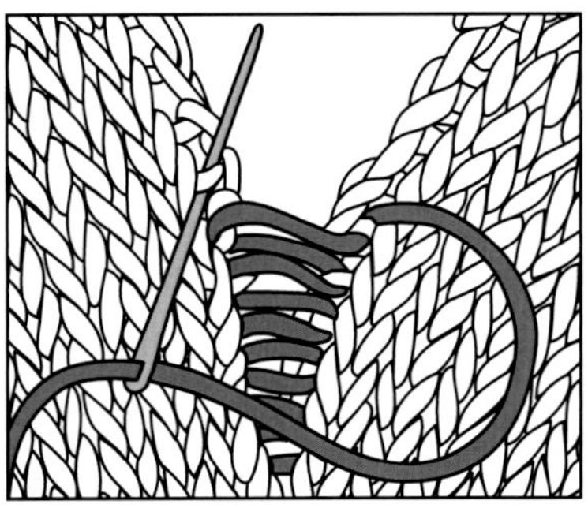

POM-POM

Cut a piece of cardboard 3" wide and as long as you want the diameter of your finished pom-pom to be. Wind the yarn around the cardboard lengthwise until it is approximately ½" thick in the middle ***(Fig. 16a)***.

Fig. 16a

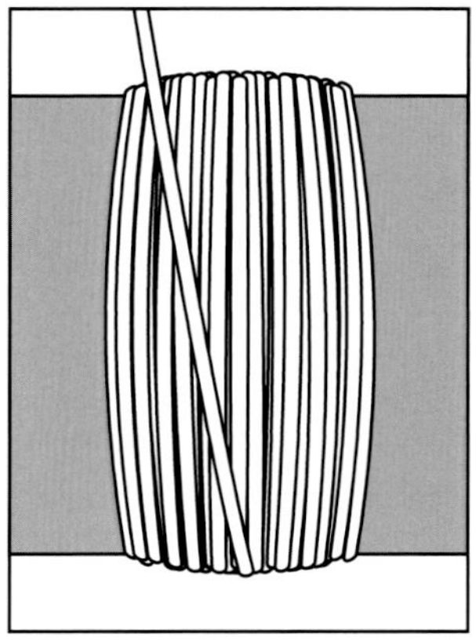

Carefully slip the yarn off the cardboard and firmly tie an 18" length of yarn around the middle ***(Fig. 16b)***. Leave yarn ends long enough to attach the pom-pom. Cut the loops on both ends and trim the porn-porn into a smooth ball ***(Fig. 16c)***.

Fig. 16b

Fig. 16c

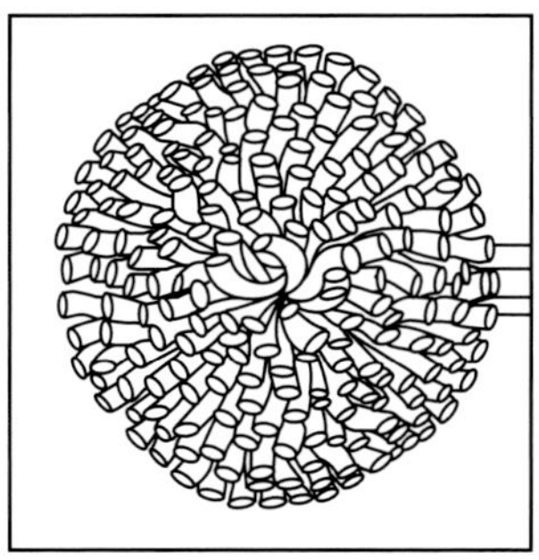

FRINGE

Cut a piece of cardboard 3" wide by 9" long. Wind the yarn **loosely** and **evenly** around the cardboard lengthwise until the card is filled, then cut across one end; repeat as needed.
Hold together 8 strands of yarn; fold in half.
With **wrong** side facing and using a crochet hook, draw the folded end up through a stitch and pull the loose ends through the folded end ***(Fig. 17a)***; draw the knot up **tightly** ***(Fig. 17b)***. Repeat, spacing evenly across short edges of Afghan.
Lay flat on a hard surface and trim the ends.

Fig. 17a

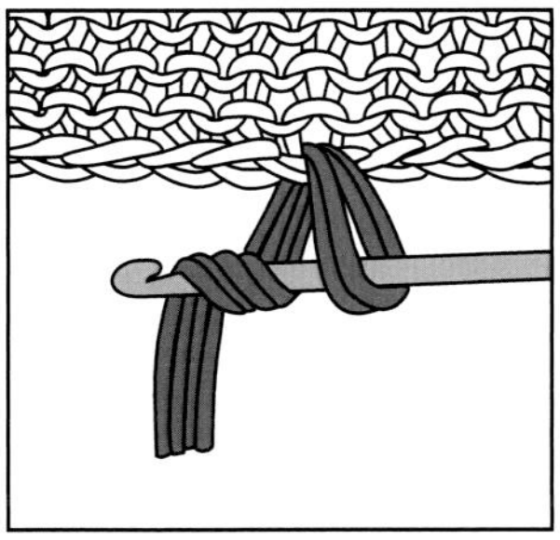

Fig. 17b

CROCHET STITCHES

CHAIN *(abbreviated ch)*

Bring the yarn over the hook from back to front and draw through loop on hook ***(Fig. 18)***.

Fig. 18

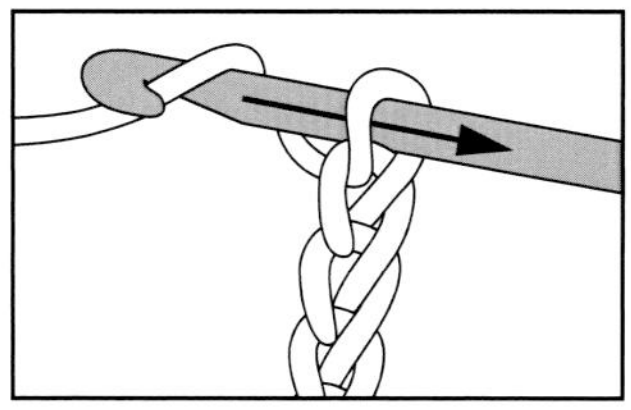

SLIP STITCH *(abbreviated slip st)*

Insert hook in stitch indicated, YO and draw through stitch and loop on hook ***(Fig. 19)***.

Fig. 19

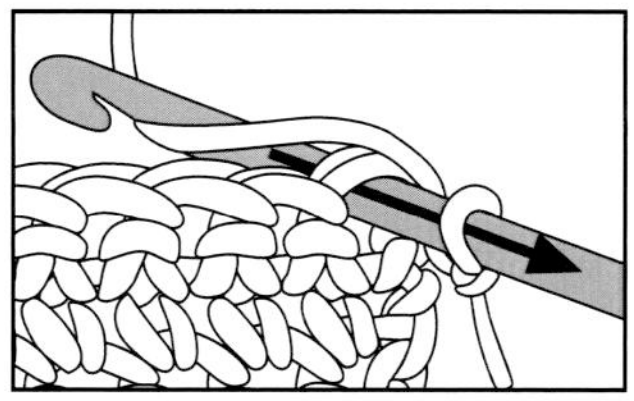

SINGLE CROCHET *(abbreviated sc)*

Insert hook in stitch or space indicated, YO and pull up a loop, YO and draw through both loops on hook ***(Fig. 20)***.

Fig. 20

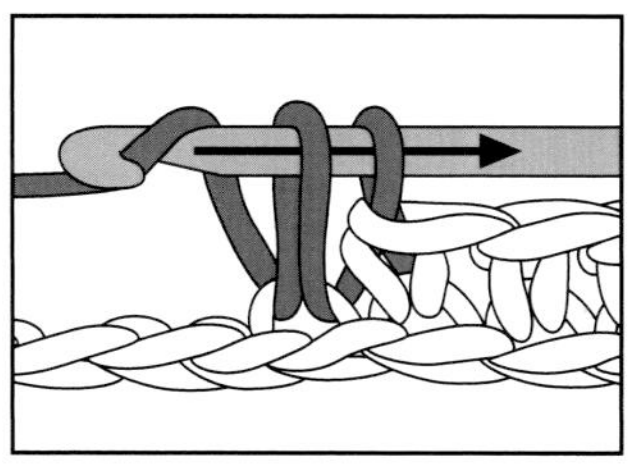

Projects made and instuctions tested by JoAnn Bowling, June Clevenger, Kay Meadors, Kitty Jo Pietzuch, Donna Soellner, Margaret Taverner, and Carol Thompson.

We have made every effort to ensure that these instructions are accurate and complete. We cannot, however, be responsible for human error, typographical mistakes, or variations in individual work.

Made in U.S.A.